BLUE AND YELLOW DON'T MAKE GREEN

by MICHAEL WILCOX

THE SCHOOL OF COLOUR

Acknowledgements

The ideas behind this book have been with me for some time, but it took a team of very special people to turn them into printed pages.

I would particularly like to express my gratitude to Peter Riordan for his invaluable expertise, energy and patience. A most generous person.

The production team, Philippa Nikulinsky, Karen Grove, Danka Pradzynski and Lynn Callister deserve special mention, their professionalism and hard work made the project possible.

Thanks also to Bill and Rosemary Cranny for their constant help and encouragement. To Janet Rowe for her invaluable assistance and to Marian Kiely for working so hard on the overall plan.

I also wish to thank Paul Green-Armytage and Ron Price for their kind help and advice.

Finally, I must thank the most important person of all, my wife Dawn.

Without her enduring patience, hard work and support this book would not have seen the light of day.

Published by
The School of Colour
38 Carver Road
London SE24 9LT

ISBN 0 9587891 9 3

Editor
Peter Riordan

Designer
Danka Pradzynski

Illustrators
Philippa Nikulinsky
Michael Wilcox

Finished Artist
Karen Grove

Assistant Artist
Anthea Ratcliff

Typesetting
Key West Photosetting
Western Australia

Colour separations
C.H.Colour Scan Sdn.Bhd.
Kuala Lumpur, Malaysia.

Printing
Tien Wah (Malaysia) Sdn.
Bhd. Kuala Lumpur.

First published in 1987.
Reprinted 1988, 1989, 1990,
1991, 1992, 1993.
Revised edition 1994

Introduction

Colour has long aroused strong emotions. It has a powerful and direct impact on the brain giving rise to responses varying from aggression to tranquillity. There is every reason for anyone using colour to understand and take control of this very forceful means of communication.

Artists, designers, printers, craft workers and other users of colour would invariably agree that the selection and use of colour is of paramount importance in their work. And yet, despite growing interest in colour's potential, a great deal of misunderstanding surrounds colour mixing.

As children we are told that there are three colours - the primaries - which can be mixed to make all other colours. The teacher provides a red, yellow and blue and we quickly find that we can mix them and obtain further colours.

(We also find that it is very easy to mix a colour usually described as 'mud').

Those of us who become further involved find this approach too limiting, we desire a wider range of colours to cater for our more sophisticated requirements.

Yet it seems that however many colours we purchase and whatever we read on the subject, at the end of the day it still remains very much a hit and miss affair.

The need to be able to mix any desired result quickly, accurately and without waste is readily apparent but unfortunately very few are able to do this. Even after many years of experience most people find difficulty in mixing colours.

Are there reasons for these difficulties? Can they be overcome?

I believe that the three primary system on which we rely so heavily has in fact created many of the stumbling blocks to mastering colour mixing. It is a very rough, crude guide which offers help with one hand and takes it away with the other.

The problems associated with colour mixing can be overcome but first we need to discard the notion of primary colours and replace it with a more up-to-date conceptual framework.

Michael Wilcox

The School of Colour

Reaction to the first editions of this book led to further research and consultation with artists, designers, printers, craft workers and educationalists.

The result has been the formation of a School of Colour.

The School is concerned, first and foremost, with the supply of accurate and useful information aimed at removing the many barriers to creativity.

Few people are able to realise their full creative potential due to the incredible confusion which surrounds most aspects of colour use.

This confusion has been compounded throughout this century and we now find ourselves, near the year 2000, with less understanding of this vital area than the Impressionists of the 1800s.

The intention of the School is to remedy this situation and remove the barriers. Coming to a full understanding of the potential of colour should be both enjoyable and straightforward.

Further information on the School of Colour is given at the end of this book.

Contents

The Current Approach to Colour Mixing

The Three Primary System   7

History and Development of
the Three Primary System   12

Colour Memory   14

Colour Biases

What is Colour   15

Primary Colours   20

Inside the Paint Film   21

Mixing the Three 'Primaries'   23

Mixing just Two 'Primaries'   25

The Painters Primary Colours Do Not Exist

Pigment Colour Bias   31

Introduction to the Colour Bias Wheel   33

The Surviving Light   34

The Traditional View   36

'Primaries' and 'Secondaries'?   38

The Colour Bias Wheel   39

The Basic Palette

The Limited Palette   41

Cadmium Red Light   42

Quinacridone Violet   42

Ultramarine Blue   42

Cerulean Blue   43

Lemon Yellow   43

Cadmium Yellow Pale   43

Exploring the Basic Palette's Range

Selecting Contributing Colours   45

Exploring the Clear Colours   52

Colour Wheel A - Clear Colours   54

Neutralized Colours   55

Colour Wheel B   61

Colour Wheel C   62

Colour Wheel D   63

Deciding on Colour Type

Reds   64

Yellows and Blues   65

Greys and Neutral Colours

Greys and Neutrals from the
Complementaries 67

Yellow/Violet 69

Blue/Orange 70

Red/Green 71

Other Complementary Pairs 72

Colour Wheel E 73

Colour Wheel F 74

Transparent, Semi Transparent and Opaque Paints

Paint Films 75

Transparent Colours 77

Colour Wheel G 84

Further Transparent Colours 85

Opaque Colours 86

Colour Wheel H 86

Further Opaque Colours 87

Adding White and Black

Adding White 89

Adding Black 92

Browns

How to Make Your Own Browns 95

Manufactured Browns 96

The Palette

Summary of the Extended Palette 97

Mixing 'Standard' Colours 99

Mixing Various Media

Pastels 101

Coloured Pencils 104

Silk Screen Inks 106

Watercolours 108

Gouache 109

Oil Paints 110

Acrylics 112

Placing Further Colours 114

Subtractive Mixing in Practice 116

Further Titles 118

The School of Colour 120

The Current Approach to Colour Mixing

We must understand the inherent limitations of present methods if we are to expand our capabilities.

The Three Primary System
History and Development of the Three Primary System
Colour Memory

The Three Primary System

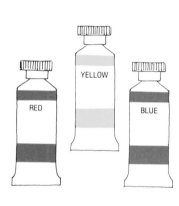
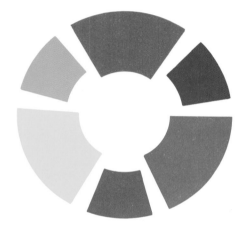

Traditionally the 'primaries' are thought of as being the base colours from which other colours are mixed but which cannot, themselves, be created from other colours.

Red, yellow and blue are the 'primaries' used in the mixing of paint, inks, pastels, coloured pencils etc.

They can be found on a great variety of colour wheels, together with the resulting 'secondary' colours: blue and yellow are shown as making green, yellow and red are shown as making orange and red and blue making violet.

On paper the system appears to work very well. All that needs to be done is to select a red, yellow and blue from the range offered and mix away.

Put to the test the three primary system seems sound enough. A green does result when blue and yellow are mixed and violet and orange can be obtained by combining other 'primary' colours.

7

The first of the problems involved with the 'three primary system' comes with the selection of the colours. Which red, yellow and blue to use? There are so many to choose from.

With so much conflicting advice being offered by books, fellow artists and teachers, painters often turn up at their art material supplier with little idea of where to start.

Typically they begin by purchasing a variety of reds, yellows and blues.

Three or four tubes of each 'primary' colour is generally considered an adequate start.

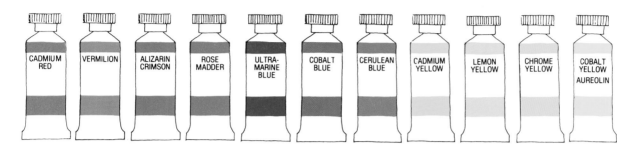

| CADMIUM RED | VERMILION | ALIZARIN CRIMSON | ROSE MADDER | ULTRA-MARINE BLUE | COBALT BLUE | CERULEAN BLUE | CADMIUM YELLOW | LEMON YELLOW | CHROME YELLOW | COBALT YELLOW AUREOLIN |

And a few other colours too, just to be sure.

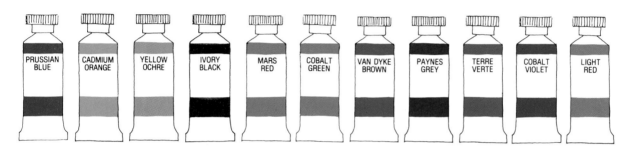

| PRUSSIAN BLUE | CADMIUM ORANGE | YELLOW OCHRE | IVORY BLACK | MARS RED | COBALT GREEN | VAN DYKE BROWN | PAYNES GREY | TERRE VERTE | COBALT VIOLET | LIGHT RED |

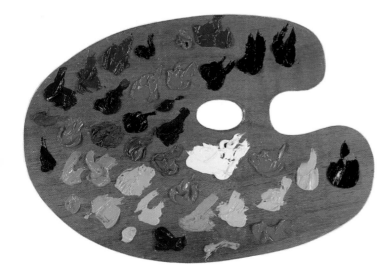

A common approach is to start by squeezing small amounts of each of the colours on to the palette. Many of the paints are used as they come from the tube, with little or no modification.

Work on the painting progresses, but there soon comes a time when a particular colour is required that is not available ready mixed. Let's say a bluish violet is wanted.

A red and blue are mixed, but the result is nowhere near the one needed.

A different red is tried. Things get worse — the mix has turned grey.

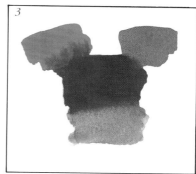

Perhaps it needs another of the many reds on the palette. No, that's worse still.

There is now a large amount of dirty grey paint — mud — on the palette. Can't discard it because paints are so expensive nowadays.

Some of the mix is scraped up and moved to a clean part of the palette.
Maybe it was the blue that was at fault.

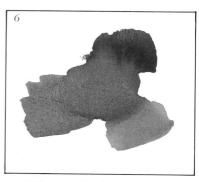

The original red is re-introduced and another blue mixed in.
It's a little bit better, but still very dull.

More of the red and blue is added to the growing mix and it starts to look more like violet.

A little yellow paint is accidently mixed in. Not to worry, it's only a tiny amount.
Suddenly the mix is worse than ever. It's become a very dark grey.

Understandable frustration sets in. The two large blobs of unwanted (and expensive) grey paint are scraped off and a fresh start is made.

The colour that is eventually used is not quite the one that was in mind but it will 'have to do'.

If this is all very familiar to you, take heart because many artists can sympathise with your predicament. They too end up using colours that are less than satisfactory, thereby severely limiting their colour expression, exhausting their patience and attaining a diminished level of satisfaction from their work.

Thanks to our present wasteful colour mixing practices, the only ones to benefit are the paint manufacturers.

Confusion arises out of the vast choice of 'secondary' colours available from the 'primaries'.

Such a wide range of greens, oranges and violets is produced that forecasting the final colour is no easy matter. They are all useful colours but how can we be sure of mixing them to order?

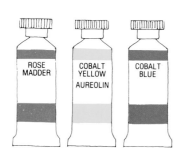

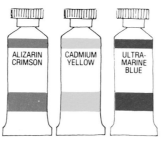

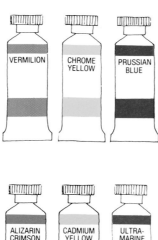

One way around the problem that is often suggested is to select just one yellow, one red and one blue and to mix all the 'secondary' colours from just these three:

ROSE MADDER

COBALT YELLOW
AUREOLIN

COBALT BLUE

VERMILION

CHROME YELLOW

PRUSSIAN BLUE

ALIZARIN CRIMSON

CADMIUM YELLOW

ULTRA-MARINE BLUE

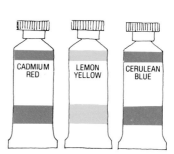

CADMIUM RED

LEMON YELLOW

CERULEAN BLUE

This combination gives clear violets but dull greens and oranges.

ALIZARIN CRIMSON CADMIUM YELLOW ULTRA-MARINE BLUE

Here the greens are bright, but the oranges are dull and the 'violets' more like dull browns.

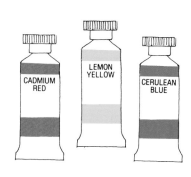

CADMIUM RED LEMON YELLOW CERULEAN BLUE

Clear oranges but very dull 'violets' and poor greens.

VERMILION CHROME YELLOW PRUSSIAN BLUE

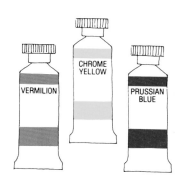

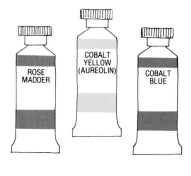

ROSE MADDER COBALT YELLOW (AUREOLIN) COBALT BLUE

These three produce better all round results, but the oranges are still dull, the violets not especially bright and all three, being transparent, look rather washed out. These colours also happen to be very costly.

Try as we might, it is impossible to find three 'primary' colours that will give us a series of clear 'secondaries'

History and Development of the Three Primary System

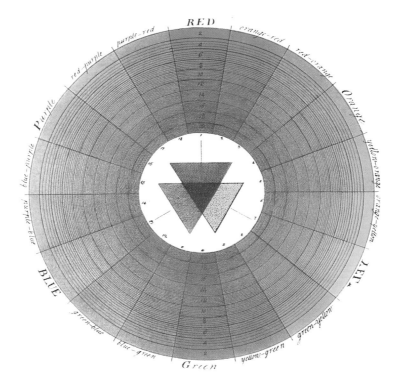

From the very earliest times, confusion has gone hand in hand with attempts to understand colour.

A multitude of interpretations have been offered about the origins and relationships of colours, but little attention has been paid to colour mixing until comparatively recently.

Surprisingly, it was not until about 1731 that the German theorist Le Blon made a discovery that many now would say should have been obvious: that a comprehensive range of colours could be obtained by using just three basic colours, red, yellow and blue.

Le Blon's discovery met with wide acclaim, one writer of the time stating "that invention has been well approv'd thro'out Europe, th'o at first it was thought impossible".

His findings were quickly embraced, particularly by the printing trade, but it was not until some forty five years later that his work was presented in a practical form.

In 1776 Moses Harris published the first organised colour wheel in an attempt to replace the then current understanding of colour, which he described as being "so dark and occult".

28 TRACT OF COLOURING.

PAINTING can *reprefent all* visible *Objects*, with three *Colours*, Yellow, Red, and Blue; for all other *Colours can be compos'd of these* Three, *which I call* Primitive; *for Example.*

Yellow
and } *make an* Orange Colour.
Red

Red
and } *make a* Purple *and* Violet
Blue } Colour.

Blue
and } *make a* Green Colour.
Yellow

And a Mixture *of those* Three *Original Colours makes a* Black, *and all other Colours whatsoever; as I have demonstrated by my Invention of* Printing *Pictures and* Figures *with their natural Colours.*

The first printed description on the nature of the 'primaries'.

He declared that red, yellow and blue — the "primitive" (primary) colours gave rise, through mixing, to the "prismatic" (secondary) colours, orange, green and violet.

And so it has remained ever since.

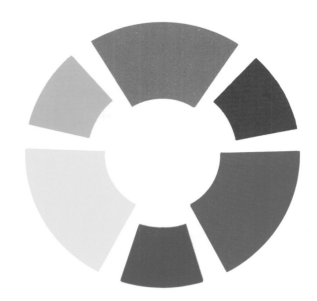

The use of the three primary system has gained universal approval and now forms the basis on which colour mixing is taught throughout the world.

The heavy reliance on this system cannot be claimed, however, to have led to generations of skilled colour mixers.

On the contrary, it has led to muddled, confused frustration.

No-one denies that the three primary system has always been clumsy to use. The difficulties are usually explained away in the following manner:

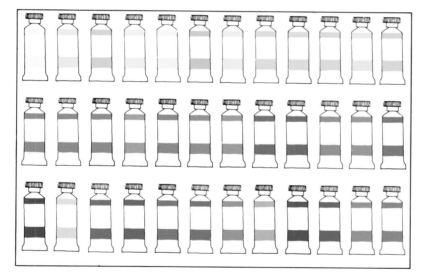

'There are so many different reds, yellows and blues on the market that it is difficult to select the exact primaries. If one took particular care in choosing them, only the three tubes of paint would ever be required.'

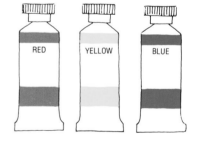

Or alternatively;

'I realise that it is not possible to obtain pure primaries in pigment form; the red is always a bit orange or violet for example, but one day such colours will probably become available and then it will be very easy to mix almost every colour imaginable'.

In both cases the belief in the three primary system is firmly entrenched.

Colour Memory

A cornerstone of the three primary system is its reliance on colour memory. Many art instruction books contain colour samples together with information on the various reds, yellows and blues that were mixed to achieve them. The reader is expected to absorb such information.

Typical advice runs along the lines: 'Mix red A with yellow B and store the result, orange C, in your memory for future use'.

Although individuals vary in their ability to recall colours accurately, we are, on the whole, equipped with a relatively poor colour memory. If you have ever tried matching up a piece of material or paint sample in a shop with the colour of your curtains or living room wall you will realise the difficulties from first-hand experience.

This is a rather extreme example, though not an uncommon one. It is almost as difficult to match up colours from memory when they are directly in front of us.

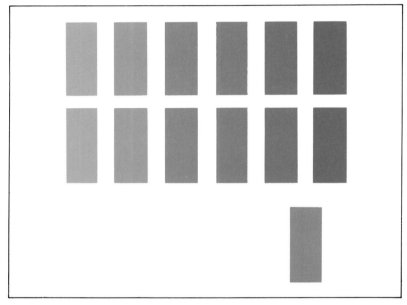

Take a dozen pieces of paper of the same hue, all slightly different greens say.

If you have another sample that matches up with one of them, you will in all probability have to resort to butting the pieces together to obtain a match unless the differences are glaringly obvious.

In the split second that it takes to look from the sample to one of the twelve choices, the image of the first colour will fade considerably. It is only when the two pieces are put side by side that we can circumvent our reliance on colour memory.

The simple fact is that we quickly forget all but the most general features of a colour as soon as we look away from it, and yet, the very foundation of colour mixing instruction relies on remembering the results of countless colour mixes.

Our colour memory certainly helps us achieve very general results but it is quickly overwhelmed attempting a fuller repertoire.

This approach, then, is unwieldy and unworkable and even years of experience mixing colours does not reverse that fact because we must still rely on an unreliable colour memory.

Colour

Understanding colour and the processes at work within the paint film transforms colour mixing into a controlled thinking process.

What is Colour?
Primary Colours
Inside the Paint Film
Mixing the Three "Primaries"
Mixing Just Two "Primaries"

What is Colour?

Where is the apple's "redness"?

Is it in the skin of the apple?

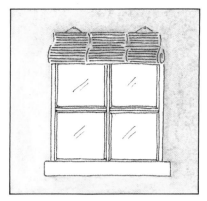

In the light coming through the window?

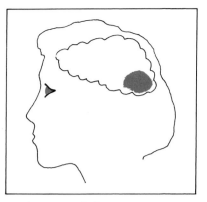

In the eye of the viewer, or in the brain?

Light

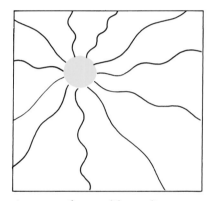

A range of wave-like radiations is emitted by the sun.

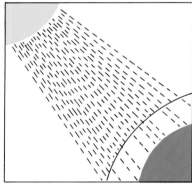

The atmosphere protects us from many of these radiations whilst allowing others to pass.

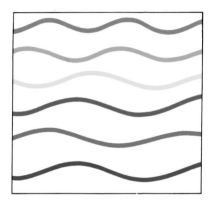

White light is made up of a series of 'colour wavelengths'.

The sun emits a variety of wave-like radiations, each of which can be thought of as similar to a rope being shaken at one end. (This is a very simplified explanation).

Many of these radiations, known as electromagnetic waves, are prevented by the atmosphere from reaching the earth. X-rays, infra-red rays and light rays are among those electromagnetic waves which do penetrate the atmosphere.

The visible light that reaches the earth is made up of wavelengths that, although similar in character, vibrate at slightly different speeds or frequencies. Varying light wavelengths represent different colours and together they reach us in the form of white light.

For the sake of clarity they are shown here in colour. While they remain part of the light they cannot be seen.

This white light is the natural light we call daylight. Since the various colour wavelengths that constitute daylight are travelling in a combined form, they must be broken down, or decoded, if they are not to remain simply as white light.

The Prism

One way of separating the individual colours is to pass the light through a prism.

When light strikes an angled surface it is deflected slightly from its path. In the case of a glass prism, the light bends but continues its journey. Each of the various wavelengths that make up white light are bent at slightly different angles.

Because the wavelengths are bent by differing amounts as they pass through the prism, they become separated from their travelling companions. If a white card is put in their path, the full colours of the spectrum are revealed.

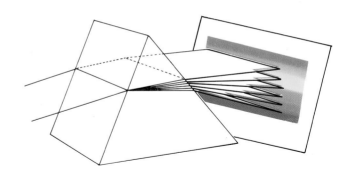

Through his work with the prism, Newton was able to prove that all colours are physically contained within white light.

Surface Colour

The colours contained in natural or artificial light can be made visible if the light strikes a surface.

But why do surfaces reveal different colours when they are struck by the same white light? The answer is due to the nature of matter and the fact that, like X-rays and infra-red radiation, light is a form of energy.

The make-up of matter:

Every object is made up of atoms which are seething with invisible energy. Electrons are in constant orbit around their centres or nuclei.

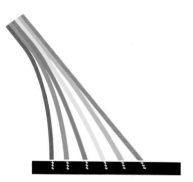

A black surface will absorb the energy of the light

The energy contained in white light is often compatible with the energy within a surface and when that happens, they merge. The energy within the surface absorbs the energy within the light.

Exactly what happens when light strikes a surface depends on the molecular make-up of that surface.

Some surfaces efficiently absorb all the different 'colour waves', reflecting very little back. Such surfaces appear black. The energy contained in the light which a black surface absorbs is turned into heat.

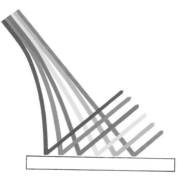

A white surface on the other hand, has a molecular make-up that rejects or reflects almost all 'colour waves' equally. The 'colour waves' therefore remain as white light.

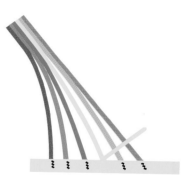

A yellow surface absorbs nearly all 'colour waves' except the yellow which is rejected and reflected back from the surface to our eyes. As we can now only see the reflected yellow portion of the light, the object appears to be yellow. The other 'colour waves' have been absorbed and turned into heat.

Since all the 'colour waves' contained in the white light arrived at the surface at the same time, the 'yellow waves' are reflected over the entire surface area.

If a surface appears blue, it follows that the other 'colour waves' — the red, orange, yellow, green and violet — have been absorbed into the surface and the 'blue waves' reflected back to the eye.

When we describe a flower as being red, what we are really describing is that part of the light left after the rest has been subtracted. The molecular make-up of its surface is such that it absorbs every light ray except the red. The flower ITSELF does not somehow possess the red. The colour is generated ONLY by the light falling on it.

It is not only single colours that are reflected: a yellow-green leaf reflects varying proportions of both yellow and green.

The colour that the viewer eventually receives, therefore, is the remnant or residue of the light that arrived at the surface. The rest has been absorbed.

The hues of the spectrum are reflected in various combinations to produce the immense range of colours we see about us.

Colour Sensation

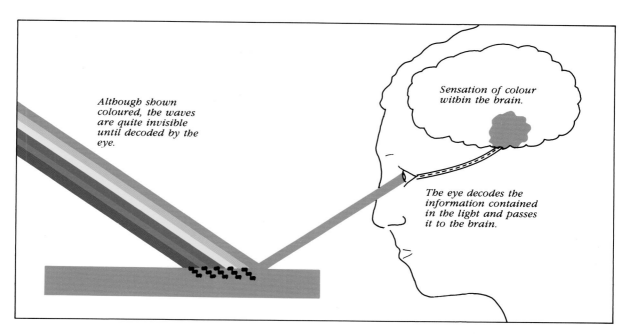

Although shown coloured, the waves are quite invisible until decoded by the eye.

Sensation of colour within the brain.

The eye decodes the information contained in the light and passes it to the brain.

We should think of the various 'colour waves' as carriers of information. Information the eye can process into a form which is suitable for the brain to make use of.

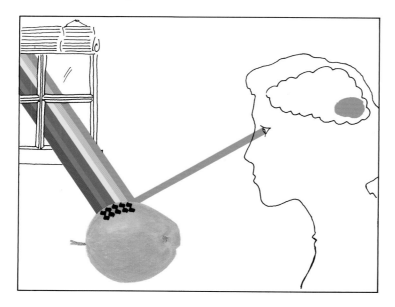

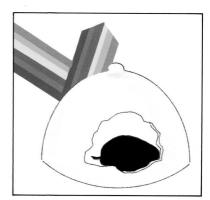

To return to the question of the apple's colour, we can now say that the redness was carried through the window in the light, that it was reflected from the skin of the apple (after losing its travelling companions), that it travelled as a code to the eye and was then passed to the brain, where it was turned into a sensation of redness.

If the apple is now covered over, it is no longer red. Without light its true colour is black. It can only appear red when the red 'colour waves' contained in the light are present.

Primary Colours

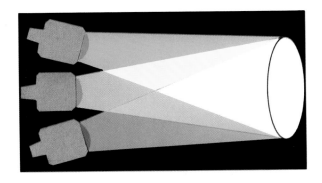

There are other sets of primary colours we should know about in addition to the traditional artist's primaries of red, yellow and blue.

Additive Primaries

The primaries of light, orange-red, green and violet-blue, combine to form white light when they are all at the correct relative luminance.

They are known as ADDITIVE primaries because when they are mixed, light is ADDED. Red and green for example make yellow, which is lighter than either the red or the green.

Psychological Primaries

First proposed by Leonardo da Vinci, the psychological or perceptual primaries are those colours that do not appear to involve any other colour. The colours red, yellow, blue and green all appear to be quite unlike each other. We cannot see, for example, any red in yellow or any blue in red.

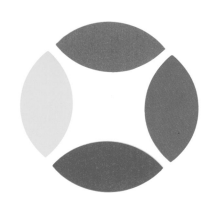

Subtractive Primaries

Red, yellow and blue are the subtractive primaries traditionally used in paint, ink and dye mixing.

They are known as SUBTRACTIVE primaries due to the fact that colours that are mixed from them become darker as light is removed, or subtracted.

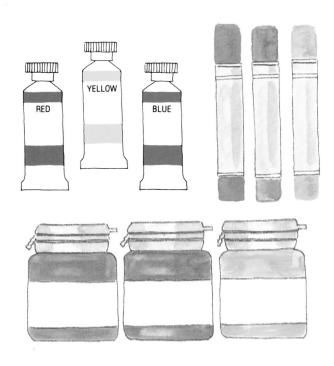

20

Inside the Paint Film

In order to understand subtractive mixing and how it can best be employed by the painter, we need to study the processes actually taking place within the paint film.

Our poor colour memory does not allow us to learn very much from the surface appearance of colours.

Consider the events which take place when light strikes a surface: a surface painted, for example, with red oil paint has a molecular make-up which

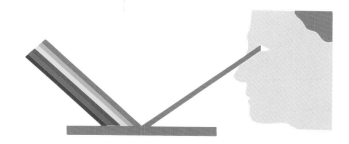

absorbs all 'colour' lightwaves and turns them into energy,

with the exception of the 'red' lightwaves which are rejected.

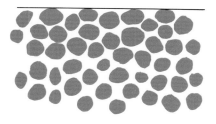

Pigments, the colouring matter of paints, are tiny particles which reflect certain colours very efficiently.

A cross section of the layer of red oil paint would look very much like this. Each tiny speck of pigment is surrounded by a binding substance, the vehicle which holds the pigment particles together to form a paint. It also provides the adhesion to hold the paint onto the painting surface. Gum is the binder in water colours, linseed oil in oil paints, etc.

Let us now isolate just one of the pigment particles and consider what takes place when light arrives at its surface.

The red light reflected from just one tiny particle would be difficult to see, but combine thousands of such particles and the collective red light becomes easily discernible.

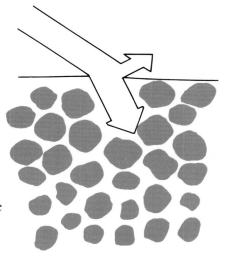

There is one other factor to consider. When oil is used as the binder, as in this case, it forms a smooth film and acts as a rather efficient reflector of light. So some light is bounced straight off.

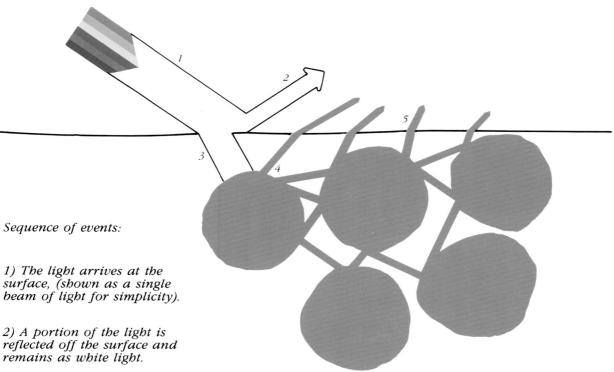

Sequence of events:

1) The light arrives at the surface, (shown as a single beam of light for simplicity).

2) A portion of the light is reflected off the surface and remains as white light.

3) Much of the light continues on its journey and enters the oil binder, (which is clear and glassy in fresh paint).

4) When the light reaches the pigment particles, most of it is absorbed, apart from the red portion which is reflected.

Pigments absorb the majority of every other colour except their own.

5) The reflected red light either leaves the binding film directly or bounces off other pigment particles, before finally emerging from the paint film.

This red light combines with the reflected white light, giving an overall brighter effect.

Via the eye, this information is recorded as a red 'sensation' within an observer's brain.

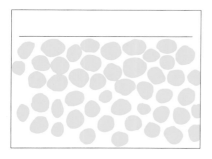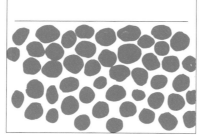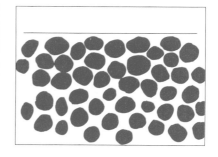

Yellow particles in a layer of yellow paint would each be reflecting a tiny amount of yellow light.

Each tiny speck of pigment in a film of blue paint would reflect a tiny amount of that colour.

If the paint appeared green it would be due to the collective green light being reflected from the pigment particles.

Mixing the Three "Primaries"

Now that the basic mechanics of the paint film have been examined we can consider the processes within the paint layer when we physically mix colours.

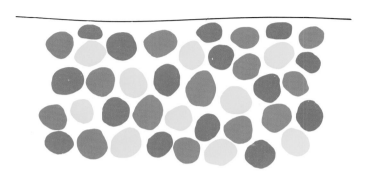

We will learn a great deal by mixing the traditional painter's 'primaries' and examining why the result is a grey, almost black colour.

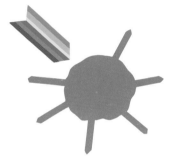

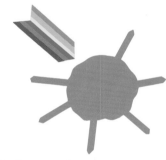

1. Light that strikes the yellow pigment in the mix is absorbed apart from the yellow which is reflected.

2. Light arriving at the blue pigment is destroyed in the same way, with the exception of its blue component which is 'bounced off'.

3. Every colour contained in the light, with the exception of red, is absorbed by the red pigment.

We have just seen that red, yellow and blue pigments convert the light into red, yellow and blue light respectively. But where do these coloured lights go from there? Deep within the paint film their options are limited.

If the yellow light reflected by the yellow pigment happens to meet up with another yellow particle, it is reflected again and is therefore temporarily safe.

If, however, it strikes a blue or red speck of pigment, it is absorbed.

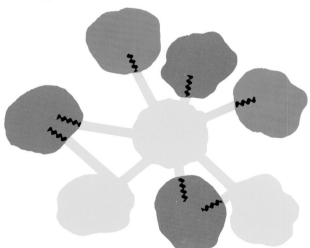

Suddenly, there is no more yellow light.

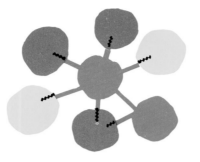 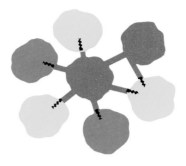

In the case of the blue light reflected by the blue pigment, it too can bounce off other blue particles, but is absorbed by either the red or the yellow. No more blue!

Similarly the red light will soon become absorbed by the blue and yellow. Goodbye red light!

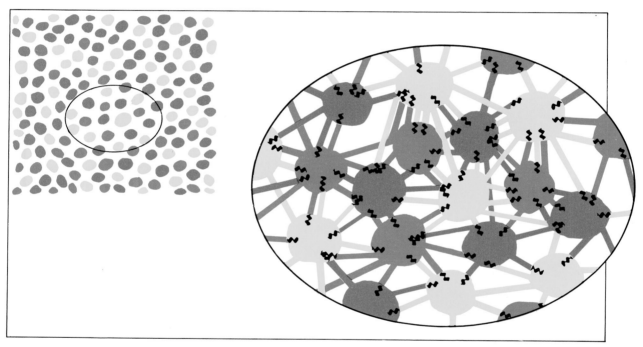

All the white light which initially sank into the paint was absorbed, except the blue, yellow and red. When they in turn are absorbed, what is left? The simple answer is — nothing.

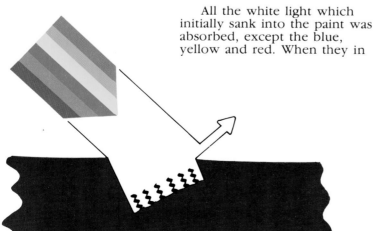

The conclusion, therefore, is that if the three traditional SUBTRACTIVE 'primaries' are mixed in equal INTENSITIES, only a minute proportion of the light energy reaching the surface is reflected, while the rest is absorbed. The result is a very dark grey, approaching black.

At this point a useful exercise would be to mix such a dark. Combine any red, yellow and blue.

Start by mixing the three in roughly equal proportions. Do not be concerned if you cannot obtain a dark straight away, since paints can vary enormously in intensity of colour.

Thin a portion of the mix near its edge to see if one or even two of the 'primaries' are dominating. If they are, add small amounts of the colour or colours being swamped until you have a dark, blackish grey. If at first the result is an orange, add blue; if it leans towards violet, add yellow; and if greenish, add red.

By mixing the three subtractive 'primaries' in near equal intensities so much incoming light is destroyed that very little escapes.

Mixing just Two 'Primaries'

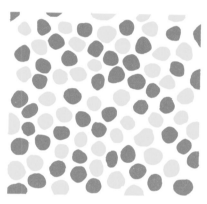

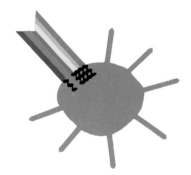

If just two PURE 'primary' colours were to be mixed, the result would be most unexpected. Take the example of a PURE yellow and a PURE blue.

Here the yellow pigment absorbs all light except the yellow.

The blue pigment likewise absorbs all but the blue portion of the light.

The next event in the sequence is that the yellow pigment absorbs all the blue light and vice-versa and the result is a **dark grey, almost black.**

But how can this be? Everyone knows that blue and yellow paint make green.

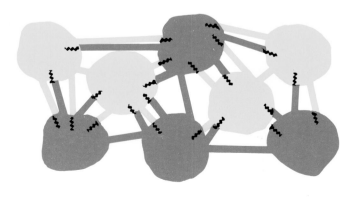

BLUE AND YELLOW DO
NOT MAKE GREEN

This may seem a rather wild statement to make, but in fact it sets the stage for a REAL understanding of colour mixing.

In this example of mixing blue and yellow, the word PURE was emphasised, PURE yellow and PURE blue.

Two such pure 'primaries' WOULD make a vary dark grey, almost a black.

The mix was in fact theoretical because we do not, as yet, have pigments that are pure in hue. There is no such substance as a yellow paint which reflects only 'yellow' wavelengths.

Nor do we have a blue paint that is entirely pure.

Yellow and Red

Again we will follow the same reasoning that gave us black from the three 'primaries'.

This time another pair of 'primaries' will be mixed, pure red and pure yellow.

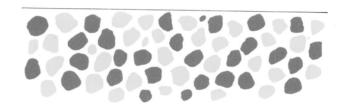

Traditional colour mixing theory tells us that red and yellow will combine into a new colour - orange.

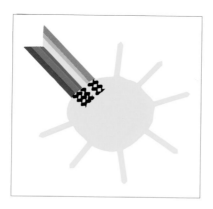 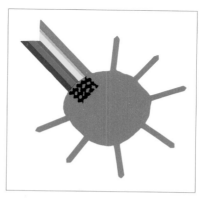

The yellow pigment in the mix will absorb the red, orange, green, blue and violet parts of the light and reflect only the yellow.

Similarly the red pigment will absorb all colours but red, which is reflected.

The light which arrives at the surface of the paint is converted into yellow and red light. These two colours then absorb each other. Red pigment will of course absorb yellow light and the yellow will destroy the red.

It can confidently be stated that yellow and red make black.

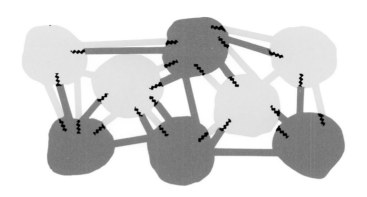

Red and Blue

Once again we can make a journey into the paint film.

A cross section of a mixture of red and blue would look very much like this.

In practice the pigment would be packed a little tighter together, but the basic structure would remain the same.

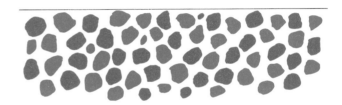

Once you are familiar with visualising a paint mix from the inside, you will be half way to controlling the final result.

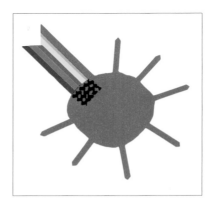

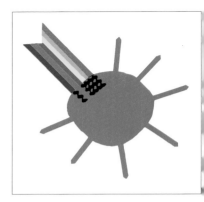

The red pigment only appears that colour to us because it is able to reflect red light and absorb colours such as blue.

The specks of blue pigment will reflect blue light but absorb all other colours.

You will be well ahead of me by now and have worked out just why a mix of pure blue would produce black.

The flaws in our traditional way of thinking about colour mixing are starting to show.

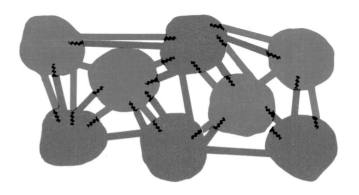

The so called 'secondary' colours, green, violet and orange must obviously come from somewhere.

Before moving on to discover the source of these colours, it is important to realise that they do not

actually materialise from a combination of the 'primaries' as such. *New* colours are not formed at all.

The Painters' Primary Colours Do Not Exist

The present system is unable to cope — it leads to frustration, limited colour expression and an enormous waste of expensive paint. There is a simple answer: that is, to abandon the three primary system and replace it with an entirely different way of viewing colours — we have to change the way that we think.

Pigment Colour Bias

Introduction to the Colour Bias Wheel

The Surviving Light

The Traditional View

'Primaries' and 'Secondaries'?

Pigment Colour Bias

Of all the pigments available to the painter, none can be described as being absolutely pure in hue. There is simply no such thing as a pure red, yellow or blue paint.

Paints may appear as a single hue and are often described as pure, but this is inaccurate.

When we first looked at why an object appeared a certain colour, we did so in a simplified form. Let us now go back in more detail.

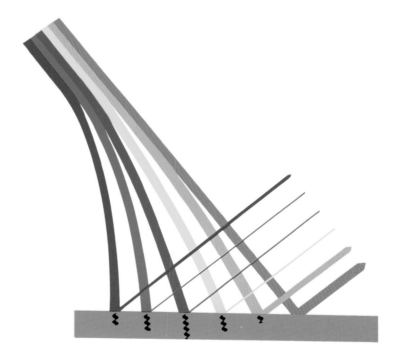

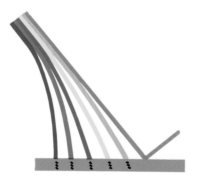

Up until now, we have said that a colour such as say, Cadmium Red, is created by the surface absorbing every colour except its own, in this case red.

In reality the majority of the red portion of light escapes, BUT SO TOO WILL VARYING AMOUNTS OF EVERY OTHER COLOUR CONTAINED IN THE LIGHT.

The red light is reflected together with a relatively large amount of the orange light. Some yellow escapes and a small amount of green, blue and violet. Every spectrum colour is represented in the final colour that we perceive.

The two major components reflected are red and orange, while the rest of the colours are found in relatively tiny amounts.

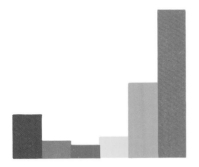

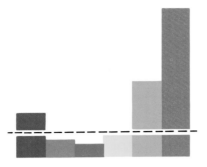

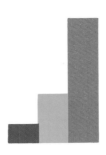

This is another way to demonstrate the content of reflected colours; the columns represent in an approximate way the 'stray' colours reflected along with the red from a layer of Cadmium Red paint.

If we were to draw a line through the chart, we could basically say that all colours below it leave in the form of white light, since an equal amount of each spectral colour produces white light.

The remaining colours of any significance are red followed by orange and violet.

4

This diagram represents, in a simplified way, the colours reflected from a layer of Cadmium Red paint.

5

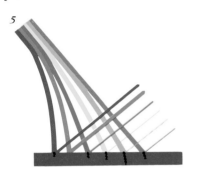

6

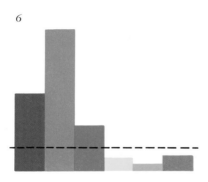

7

Other paint colours can be similarly described. Ultramarine Blue for example

is a pigment which strongly reflects blue as well as some

violet and a small amount of green.

The six basic mixing colours soon to be introduced can be analysed as follows:

Cadmium Red Light - red, orange and a small amount of violet.

Quinacridone Violet - red, plus violet and a touch of orange.

Ultramarine Blue - reflect. blue, some violet and a little green.

Cerulean Blue - blue with lesser amounts of green and violet.

Lemon Yellow - yellow, some green and a little orange.

Cadmium Yellow - yellow, some orange and to a lesser extent green.

Introduction to the Colour Bias Wheel ©

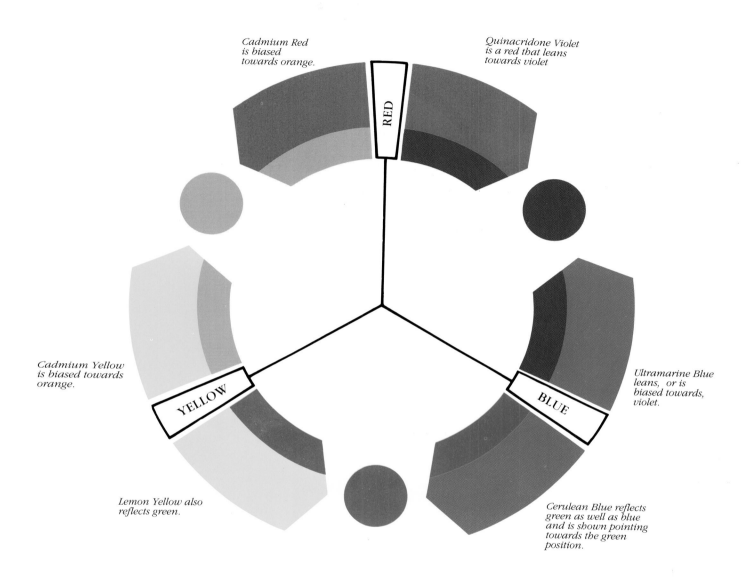

Cadmium Red is biased towards orange.

Quinacridone Violet is a red that leans towards violet

RED

Cadmium Yellow is biased towards orange.

YELLOW

BLUE

Ultramarine Blue leans, or is biased towards, violet.

Lemon Yellow also reflects green.

Cerulean Blue reflects green as well as blue and is shown pointing towards the green position.

To simplify matters at this stage, we need only consider the two main colours involved. Don't forget about the third colour though because it will reappear later.

(Such a 'third' colour would be the green in the Ultramarine Blue. See previous page).

The two reds, yellows and blues that we have just analysed (page 32), adopt these positions when formed into the 'Colour Bias Wheel'. As the name implies, the wheel indicates the leaning or bias of each colour.

As you will discover, further colours can be placed onto the Bias Wheel. Vermilion is also an orange-red for example.

It is suggested that you refer to this diagram whilst studying the next two pages.

The Surviving Light

Green

Cerulean Blue

Lemon Yellow

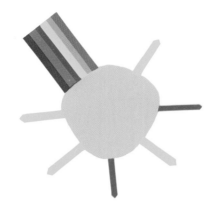

We have already found that if a PURE yellow and a PURE blue were mixed they would result in a dark grey, not a green.

Let's now examine very closely what happens when IMPURE yellow and blue pigments are mixed, for this example Lemon Yellow and Cerulean Blue.

Broadly speaking we can say that Lemon Yellow absorbs all colours in the light except yellow and a certain amount of green. The Cerulean Blue reflects blue and also some green.

For now we will ignore the small amount of orange in the yellow and the violet in the blue.

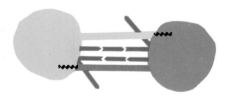

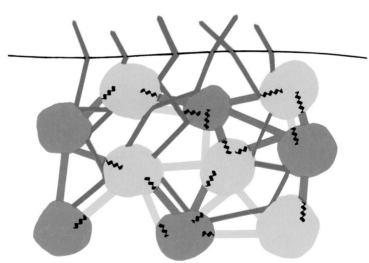

The yellow and the green reflected by the Lemon Yellow pigment are treated quite differently as they strike the Cerulean Blue. The yellow is absorbed because a blue surface absorbs yellow. But the green is reflected because here we have a type of blue which also reflects green. Cerulean Blue pigment reflects both blue and green light and when the two arrive together at the yellow particles, the blue is absorbed, (as yellow destroys blue) but the green is reflected because Lemon Yellow is a type of yellow which rejects green.

Some of the green light is reflected immediately by these two colours while the remainder 'bounces' around between the blue and yellow pigments unable to find an outlet. Eventually it makes its way to the surface of the paint film and escapes.

Can you see then that the yellow and blue do not themselves mix into a green? It is simply that green is the only colour able to survive the subtractive process; and it is present because neither the yellow nor the blue were PURE 'primaries'.

Or put another way, we can say that we are able to mix green from blue and yellow because both colours carry green as an 'impurity'.

Violet

Quinacridone Violet

Ultramarine Blue

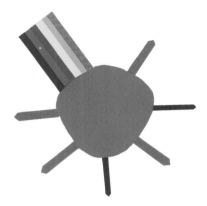

In the same way that yellow and blue do not themselves combine to form green, so red and blue do not themselves make violet.

If the blue and red both 'carry' or reflect violet, the violet will escape when the red and blue are mixed. The red and blue actually 'cancel each other out' or subtractively absorb one another in an even mix.

Orange

Cadmium Yellow

Cadmium Red

Similarly a mix of red and yellow will only produce orange if they both carry orange as an 'impurity'. Pure red and pure yellow, if we had them, would be quite incapable of producing an orange.

The Traditional View

Having established that pure 'primaries' do not exist and that even if they did, they would only result in black when mixed, traditional colour mixing wheels start to look inadequate and antiquated.

The subtractive 'primaries' have been given pride of place on countless colour wheels, as if these colours actually existed. We now know that they do not exist, either in pigment form or in nature.

For this reason the red, yellow and blue positions have been left blank in the colour bias wheel on page 33. We have neither paint, ink, nor dye with which to colour them.

Definitions of a Primary Colour

Red, yellow and blue are commonly described as being 'primary' in nature because (1) they cannot be mixed from other colours and (2) through mixing they produce all other colours.

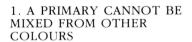

As we have made use of them for so long, we should examine these definitions.

1. A PRIMARY CANNOT BE MIXED FROM OTHER COLOURS

True, neither red, yellow or blue can be mixed from any combination of other colours. But neither, for example, can green. It has to be carried almost as an 'impurity' by the yellow and blue. Similarly orange and violet have to be introduced by the 'primaries'. They are all equally independent as they too cannot be mixed from other colours.

When we mix a green, we SAY that we are producing it from blue and yellow. It would certainly seem to be the case that yellow and blue combine to give a new colour.

For what seemed like perfectly logical reasons we have relegated green, violet and orange to the position of 'secondary' colours.

If we define a primary as a colour that cannot be mixed from others, then with our new information, we are compelled to include green, violet and orange.

To define red, yellow and blue as primaries is only true in a rough and ready way — leading to rough and ready colour mixing skills.

2. THROUGH MIXING THE PRIMARIES, ALL OTHER COLOURS CAN BE PRODUCED.

Again, this is patently incorrect.

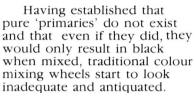

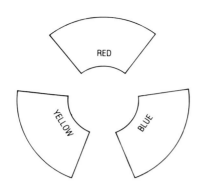

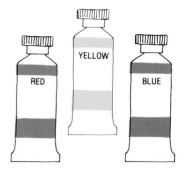

It all stems from the fact that the 'primaries' have been considered as being pure colours — whereas in fact such colours do not exist. We might think that we can imagine what they would look like, but as yet we have not seen them. They are only ideas.

To go back to page 13 and the present thinking behind the primary system of colour mixing:

• If the red, yellow and blue were chosen carefully all would be fine — but this is obviously not the case.

• One day the paint manufacturers will give us really pure primaries and then we will be able to produce a complete range from one tube each of red, yellow and blue.

If the day ever does arrive when we discover pigments that only reflect a very limited range of 'colour waves', they will be virtually useless for mixing purposes since we will only ever get darks from them.

The Printers' Primaries

It is easy to see how the three primary system has survived for so long. As a basis from which to proceed it appears to be quite logical and has certainly been better than no system at all.

The printing industry long ago decided on its own set of primaries:

Magenta — a red leaning towards violet.
Cyan — a greenish blue.
Yellow — without a strong leaning either way.

In terms of the widest range of colour mixes that will result from the minimum number of coloured inks, these 'primaries' (with the

addition of black), are certainly most successful. Unfortunately the actual range of colours that they can produce is limited. Mixed oranges, for example, are always dull and the range is restricted in other areas.

To compensate for these limitations the printer is compelled to introduce additional colours if the range needs to be extended.

'Primaries' and 'Secondaries'?

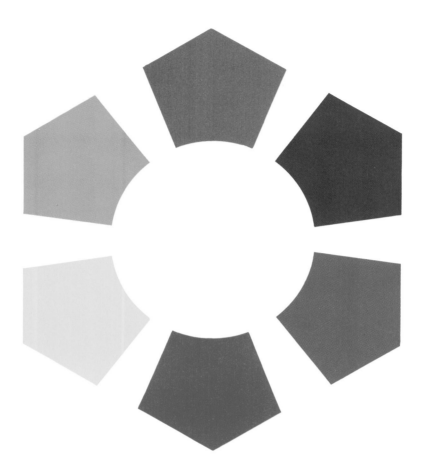

To recap briefly.

Pure primary colours do not exist.

Every red is either a violet-red or an orange-red.

Blues are either violet-blue or green-blue.

All yellows have to be either green-yellow or orange-yellow.

We can analyse the make up of these colours and depict them on a mixing guide.

Reliance on the traditional three primary system has failed to give real guidance to anyone.

But there is a simple answer: abandon the three primary system and replace it with an entirely different way of thinking about colour.

By treating the above colours on an equal basis rather than defining them as primaries and secondaries and by taking into account their presence in a mix, we can make logical decisions about selecting colours to mix.

If, for example, we no longer think of the 'primaries' yellow and blue producing the 'secondary' green, but how much green is being carried by a particular yellow and blue we can make dramatic improvements in our colour mixing results. In this example the green content must be given as much importance as the blue and yellow - and even more thought.

For too long now we have emphasised the selected of contributing colours to the exclusion of any examination of why particular results emerge.

The Colour Bias Wheel

*The leanings or biases of "primary" colours
determine the type of colour we finally mix.
To recognise and understand them is to
manipulate colour with total control.*

Colour Bias
The Bias Wheel in Action

Colour Bias

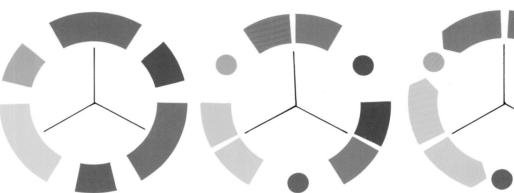

The traditional 'three primary wheel' is of limited value as it suggests the existence of colours that simply are not available, ie, one red, one yellow and one blue which together will give good, clear, predictable 'secondary colours'.

Let's stay with the basic format but use two 'types' of red, an 'orange' red and a 'violet' red; two blues, a 'violet' blue and a 'greenish' blue, and two yellows, one an 'orange' yellow and the other a 'slightly greenish' yellow.

The diagram can be further modified by forming the colours into arrows, arrows that point either towards or away from the 'secondaries'.

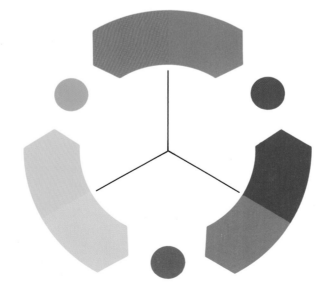

The final diagram, which we will call the COLOUR BIAS WHEEL, shows the six colour 'types' that will be used throughout this book to replace the traditional three colours.

They are an orange-red, a violet-red, a violet-blue and a green-blue, a green-yellow and an orange-yellow. These six are the MINIMUM number of colours needed for a wide selection. Each of the colour types leans or is biased towards a 'secondary' colour, as shown by the arrows.

orange-red

violet-red

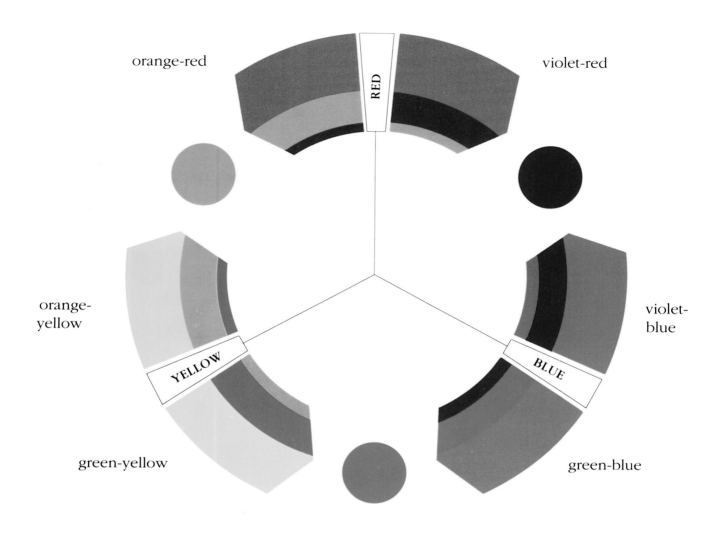

RED

orange-
yellow

violet-
blue

YELLOW

BLUE

green-yellow

green-blue

The Colour Bias Wheel, which is central to this method of working can be viewed in different ways.

On the previous page the six colour types were shown as they appear.

On page 33 the two main colour in the make up of our

six colour types were depicted.

Here we can see the three main colour which are always reflected. The colours first described on page 32.

At the moment this diagram might look a little like a multi-coloured puzzle.

Do not let this concern you.

The diagram will very soon become familiar and you will find yoursef thinking of the make up of colours in the same way.

The Basic Palette

The palette suggested here represents the six colour types: orange-red, violet-red, violet-blue, green-blue, green-yellow and orange-yellow.

The Limited Palette

Cadmium Red Light

Quinacridone Violet

Ultramarine Blue

Cerulean Blue

Lemon Yellow

Cadmium Yellow Pale

The Limited Palette

It is not an easy matter to gain complete control of a palette consisting of even three colours, yet many start their painting career by assembling as many colours as they can. The average painter's box looks as if it would benefit from the addition of a set of wheels and an engine. This approach can only lead to confusion, and expensive confusion at that.

Rather than go all out to make the paint manufacturer happy, it is preferable to concentrate on gaining control of a more limited palette — limited in the number of contributing colours rather than the possible results.

Most of the great masters achieved the most incredible effects from very limited palettes. Their colour effects can be reproduced today by the painter with an understanding of colour mixing and use.

Built-in Confusion

The bewildering range of colours available on today's market undoubtedly causes a great deal of confusion. This situation is exacerbated by many manufacturers of artist's paints who market their products under an ever-widening list of often meaningless names.

Many painters 'feel safe' only if they have purchased as many different colours as possible. They work from boxes cluttered with a lot of quite unnecessary tubes of paint. This arrangement not only adds enormously to the cost of painting — high enough as it is — but also lulls the painter into a false sense of security. Assuming that a large range will obviate the need for much mixing, colours are used straight from the tube with little modification. The result of such an approach is work of a limited scope, often containing harsh, poorly balanced colours and is easily recognised by the trained eye as a 'tube painting'.

A good number of these paints are not 'unique' colours at all, but simple mixes that we could produce ourselves using paint of a higher quality than is usually employed in manufacturers' colours.

By using the basic palette suggested here, you will be able to mix a very extensive range of colours and have a greater control over your materials.

There are, of course, an almost unlimited number of 'basic palettes' that can be put together, but this particular selection will, I believe, give you the greatest possible range.

This palette provides the basis for a controlled approach to colour mixing. Its use depends entirely on knowing which 'type' of colour each of the six represents. Once you appreciate the significance of the 'colour types' you can apply this knowledge to any other colour you possess, whatever your medium or discipline, whether it be, for example, painting, printing, pottery, using coloured pencils or inks. The principles remain the same.

Cadmium Red Light

Pigment Red 108
A warm red, leaning towards orange.

A strong, pure, intense orange-red, opaque and durable. It possesses a fairly high tinting strength with good covering power.

Beware of cheaper, student grades labelled as Cadmium Red or Cadmium Red Hue. They usually contain inferior substitute ingredients and have an unattractive appearance. It is worth spending the extra money for the artist quality, which is always brighter and more reliable than imitations.

The correct ingredients to look out for are 'Cadmium Seleno Sulphide'. You will find that the colour tends to vary between manufacturers so choose carefully. The brighter the better.

Stable and light resistant under normal conditions, it has earned a well deserved place on many artists' palettes. Cadmium Red is gradually replacing genuine Vermilion, an inferior and expensive material prone to darkening.

Quinacridone Violet

Pigment Violet 19
A cool red, leaning towards violet.

The history of painting has been one of constant change. This change is reflected in the pigments used as well as changes to style and technique.

Just as Cadmium Red has largely replaced Vermilion on the modern artist's palette, there have been changes to the violet-reds.

Madder reds, Magentas and Carmines, which are often prone to fading were largely replaced by Alizarin Crimson.

Although this has become the standard violet red for many, it too is unreliable.

Alizarin Crimson has an unfortunate tendency to fade when applied thinly or when mixed with white.

Despite this, I used it in early editions as the standard violet-red because many colourists possessed it and alternatives were less widely available.

I can now confidently advise the use of reliable alternatives as my guide to watercolour paints is in wide use. The pigments used (in watercolours at least), have been identified.

Although often sold under fancy or trade names, Quinacridone Violet can be identified as Pigment Violet 19. (Where such information is given).

It is worth seeking out, being transparent, vibrant and above all, lightfast.

Ultramarine Blue

Pigment Blue 29
A warmish blue, biased towards violet.

Pure and durable with a high tinting strength. It needs to be used carefully, either alone or in mixes, due to its strength.

Unlike other blues which invariably have greenish undertones, Ultramarine leans towards violet. This makes it a vital tool in colour mixing.

The original Ultramarine, produced from the very expensive natural material Lapis Lazuli, was replaced after 1828 when the French Government awarded a prize to the inventor of a synthetic version which became known as French Ultramarine.

The creation of an artificial Ultramarine was a major breakthrough in the history of artist's pigments. It is an important blue, considered a necessity by many artists.

Cerulean Blue

Pigment Blue 35
A cool blue, leaning towards green.

A bright, clean, strong light blue which is often used for depicting clear sunny skies. Cerulean has a greater opacity than most other blues, which gives it good hiding power. Although dark blues will cover well, they rely on their depth of colour rather than their 'body'.

A very difficult pigment to produce, genuine Cerulean tends to be expensive. There are many substitutes available but none match the true pigment for purity and colour.

Choose carefully, the better qualities are usually excellent value for money. Once again

There are many imitations on the market.

avoid, if possible, the cheaper grades, as they are usually only a mixture of Phthalocyanine Blue and other blues. Extremely permanent, Cerulean possesses a very high degree of fastness to light.

Lemon Yellow

Pigment Yellow 3
Arylide Yellow
A cool yellow, leaning towards green.

Many of the Lemon Yellows available have the unfortunate tendency of gradually turning green, especially if they are ground in oil. For this reason you should particularly avoid Chrome Lemon and Strontium Lemon. I find the most reliable products, in order of preference, are based on Arylide, Cadmium and Barium.

A well produced Lemon made from Arylide is usually the safest. It also tends to be very clean and fairly transparent.

Transparent and delicate, a well made Lemon Yellow is a pale durable colour that retains its brightness very well.

The name is a general term used for a light, greenish yellow and is often used indiscriminately to describe such a yellow.

When purchasing this colour, it is vital that you check the ingredients used in its manufacture.

Certain Lemon Yellows will turn green.

Cadmium Yellow Pale

Pigment Yellow 35
A warm yellow, leaning towards orange.

When made well, this paint is lightfast and permanent for all mediums.

It is an intense, brilliant, pale yellow that is biased towards orange. Between this colour and the cooler Lemon Yellow lies the basic imaginary PURE yellow. Although rather expensive owing to the pigment used, its brightness and permanence make it well worth the money.

Substitutes bearing the name in their titles, such as Cadmium Yellow Pale Hue, are invariably inferior substitutes. Check that the ingredients are based on Sulphide of Cadmium.

If you do not possess Cadmium Yellow Pale or Light then the medium version, usually just called 'Cadmium Yellow' can be used. The colour bias remains the same although the results are rather stronger.

Notes on the Suggested Palette

There are great variations in the pigments used to make up paints and inks.

The colours that I have suggested for the basic palette vary in strength and opacity.

Quinacridone Violet and Ultramarine are exceedingly transparent.

Cadmium Yellow Pale is quite opaque yet its strength does allow it to be applied in thin layers.

Rather weak in tinting strength, Lemon Yellow can be thinned to give transparent coats, (particularly if it is based on Arylide).

Cadmium Red and Cerulean Blue are both fairly opaque.

My choice of colours, like any other palette, is open to criticism. However, it does give a very wide range of possible mixes, varies in transparency and is lightfast.

You will now have the necessary information to be able to change any of the suggested colours for others you might prefer.

Trial mixes will indicate the bias of any alternatives you choose. Please see pages 64 and 65 for guidance in this area.

'Pure Primaries'

There are alternatives to the colours that I have suggested that come closer to the theoretical pure 'primaries'. Typical of these are:

Rose Madder Genuine

This is perhaps slightly closer to true red than Quinacridone Violet. It is also very transparent.

Its weakness, high cost and tendency to fade put me off using it to any great extent.

Cobalt Blue

Cobalt Blue comes closer to being a pure blue than either of those given. This is because it usually does not have a strong bias either towards violet or green but represents both colours well.

It will not give such bright violets as Ultramarine or strong greens as Cerulean.

Aureolin

Aureolin, applied very thinly, is a relatively clear yellow without a strong bias in either direction.

Applied thickly, Aureolin takes on a 'heavy', leathery appearance. Weak in mixes.

Colour Index names

The Colour Index Name is an important means of identifying the pigment in a paint. It should be printed somewhere on the label. If such information is not given I would avoid the product.

Colour Index Names are often abbreviated; PIGMENT YELLOW 3 for example might be described as PY3.

Exploring the Basic Palette's Range

We will now start to explore the vast range of colours that are obtainable from our six colour types, orange-red, violet-red, violet-blue, green-blue, green-yellow and orange-yellow.

Selecting Contributing Colours
Exploring the Clear Colours
Colour Wheel A — Clear Colours
Neutralized Colours
Colour Wheel B
Colour Wheel C
Colour Wheel D

Reds, Yellows and Blues
The Exercises

Selecting Contributing Colours

Violets

   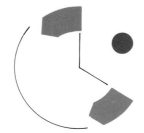

We will now start to blend various blues and reds and examine the results.

In the above, I mixed Cadmium Red Light (an orange-red), with Cerulean Blue, (a green-blue).

Although both are bright, strong colours the result is hardly a pure violet; in fact it is nearer to a dull brown, the sort of colour usually described as 'mud'.

What went wrong? After all, a blue and a red were mixed and they should have made violet.

The answer lies with the particular colours that I chose. Cadmium Red we know reflects red efficiently, orange moderately well and violet very inefficiently.

Cerulean Blue reflects blue very well and is reasonably good at reflecting green, but again is a poor performer when it comes to violet.

A break down of the Colour Bias Wheel shows that neither Cadmium Red nor Cerulean Blue was a suitable contributing colour for mixing a violet. Both point AWAY from the violet position.

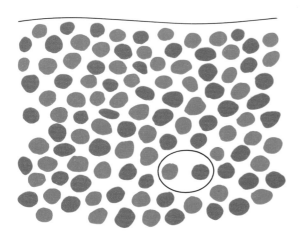

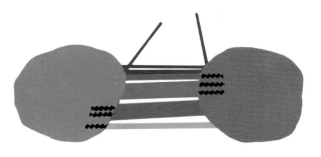

When the two paints are unleashed inside the mix they set about attacking each other's reflected lights. Cadmium Red pigment absorbs the blue and green light but reflects the small amount of violet coming from the Cerulean Blue. Cerulean Blue absorbs the red and orange but not the violet sent to it by the Cadmium Red.

The final result is a very subdued neutral with a slight leaning towards violet. It is subdued because nearly all the light entering the paint film has been absorbed and it leans towards violet because both pigments have reflected their small violet content.

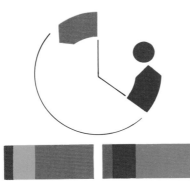

This time we will select the contributing colours a little more carefully and go for a blue which is known to be a reasonable reflector of violet, while staying with the Cadmium Red.

The blue, red, orange and green reflected by these pigments are soon absorbed, leaving only the violet. A great deal of light is lost inside this mix, but a reasonable amount of violet manages to escape. Much more so in this mix since Ultramarine Blue is an efficient reflector of violet.

The colour bias wheel predicts this result: one arrow points towards the violet position and the other points away from it.

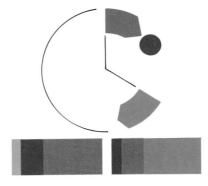

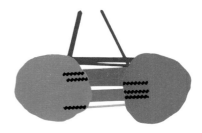

Alternatively the violet can be introduced by the red. Quinacridone Violet is a red biased towards violet.

The characteristics of the contributing colours will make changes to the resulting violet, but in both cases the colour will be subdued. Not as dull as the first mix (Cerulean Blue and Cadmium Red) but not yet bright.

46

Quinacridone Violet and Ultramarine produce one of the purest mixed violets, and for this reason:

The light that enters this mix is robbed of its blue, red, green and orange content, but the violet, which is reflected by both pigments, escapes unhindered.

All we see of the original light which entered the paint film is that part of the spectrum common to both contributing colours - violet.

As the Bias Wheel indicates, a relatively pure violet can be expected as both 'arrows' point TOWARDS the violet position.

SUMMARY

The violet colour resulting from a mixture of red and blue is essentially just the residue of the light which entered the paint film. Depending on the amount of light destroyed during the subtractive process, the final colour will be lighter or darker.

There are two factors involved in every mix, the amount of light that emerges and the colour of that light.

There is, of course, a certain amount of light reflected from the paint surface, light which does not penetrate the paint and this will lighten the result.

It should now be clear why such care must be taken with the selection of contributing colours. You will undoubtedly not be alone if you have struggled to mix a violet with just any red and blue that comes to hand.

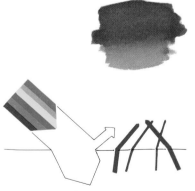

The Cadmium Red/ Cerulean Blue mix allowed very little of the incoming light to escape - giving a dull, slightly violet grey.

More violet was able to surface when either Ultramarine Blue or Quinacridone Violet were used to introduce the violet.

In the final mix the result was lighter and more violet due to the amount and nature of the light that was able to surface.

Greens

 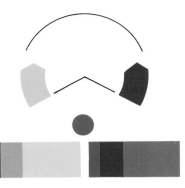 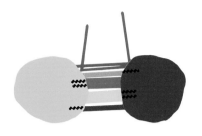

We now know in advance that a Cadmium Yellow and Ultramarine Blue mix will not result in a pure green. Both are poor, inefficient reflectors of green and in destroying nearly all of each other's colour, much of the original light striking the Ultramarine/Cadmium Yellow paint film is lost. The final colour is a very subdued grey-green; grey because very little light escapes the mix and green because that is the only surviving colour.

Again the colour bias wheel indicates the likely result; both arrows point away from the green position.

  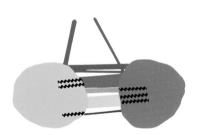

Cadmium Yellow and Cerulean Blue, by comparison, mix into a clearer green, but it is still somewhat murky as the Cadmium Yellow is not the best choice as a reflector of green. Its partner, Cerulean Blue, provides most of the green.

 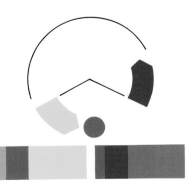 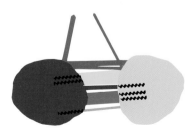

As an alternative, Lemon Yellow can be used as a means of introducing a little extra green. Still a murky green, but slightly different to the previous mix due to the different natures of the contributing colours.

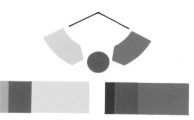

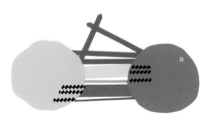

The bias wheel indicates that Lemon Yellow and Cerulean Blue are the best suited colours from our limited palette to give a clear green. Both are strong reflectors of that hue. After a certain amount of the light has been absorbed — the blue, yellow, orange and violet components — enough escapes to give both brightness and 'greenness' to the mix.

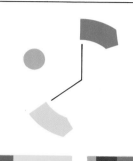

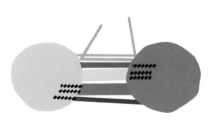

Oranges

Once again we will deliberately start with a poor selection. Neither Quinacridone Violet nor Lemon Yellow reflect very much orange. Between them, in fact, they absorb most of the light and only release a small portion which is the mutually reflected orange. The result therefore is a dull, greyed orange.

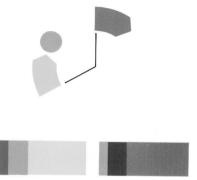

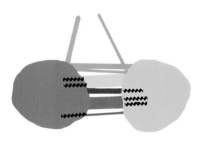

A somewhat better choice is Quinacridone Violet and Cadmium Yellow. At least the yellow can be relied on to reflect a reasonable amount of orange, but the mix is still dull because of the limited orange light able to escape.

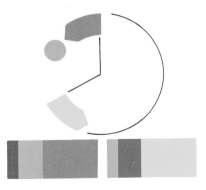

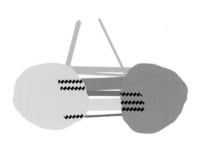

Cadmium Red will introduce orange to the mix. As the yellow used is a poor

carrier of orange, the result is still subdued.

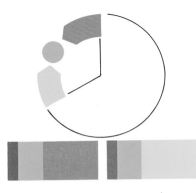

A CLEAR ORANGE

In the final exercise the contributing colours, Cadmium Red and Cadmium Yellow, have been chosen because

they are strong reflectors of orange.

The resulting bright orange represents the sole segment of the original light to survive the melee inside the paint film.

Note: The distinction between the various oranges will be more obvious if you mix them using your own paints. As mentioned elsewhere, conventional printing techniques make it difficult to highlight the differences.

Colour Mixing is a Thinking Process

The painter with an understanding of the fundamentals of subtractive mixing is in a position to obtain the desired results quickly and without wasting paint.

Once the distinctions between the different types of contributing colour are appreciated, the painter can fully control colour mixing. Now that you have taken the trouble to actually LOOK INSIDE the paint layer in order to understand the mechanics of paint mixing, you will have laid the ground work for quickly obtaining any desired colour.

Successful colour mixing is a thinking process: even if we were able to remember the results of specific colour combinations, there would be altogether just too many to absorb.

Varying the Proportions

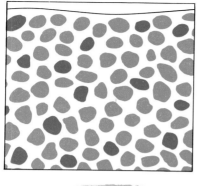

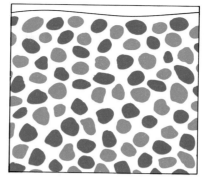

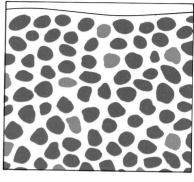

The blue is swamped by the red.

Point of equilibrium.

Now it is the turn of the red to become swamped.

The mixes that we have been studying involved two colours which were present in approximately equal proportions. We achieved a clear violet, for example, when the red and the blue were present in equal intensities. The reflected red and blue lightwaves were all absorbed, leaving only the violet.

When the proportions of the two pigments are varied, we can expect quite different reactions to take place.

If the amount of red pigment in the mix is increased, there will be insufficient blue pigment present to entirely destroy the reflected red and orange light. The result will be a red with a slight leaning towards violet. You can see this in the first few boxes of the exercise on page 52. As the blue content in that range of mixes is increased, it is able to destroy more and more of the light being reflected by the red.

About the centre of the range, a point of equilibrium is reached where all reflected light is destroyed, apart from the violet.

The mix moves towards blue as more of that colour is added. Now it is the red's turn to be swamped. More of the blue and green light reflected by the blue pigment is able to escape and mingle with the violet light. There were simply not enough particles of red pigment in the mix to physically cope with the large amounts of blue light.

A similar situation will exist wherever two (or more) colours are combined in unequal proportions. A green mixed from a combination of blue and yellow, for example, will become a blue-green if more blue paint is added, simply because the yellow pigment will not be able to destroy all of the blue light.

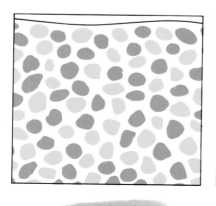

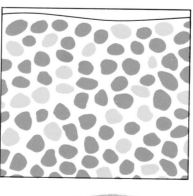

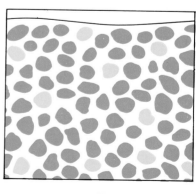

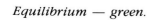

Equilibrium — green.

Moving towards blue-green.

More blue is added.

Exploring the Clear Colours

Clear Violets

In this section we will concentrate on colours in terms of their suitability to produce clear results. But bear in mind that duller mixes are no less useful and will be studied later.

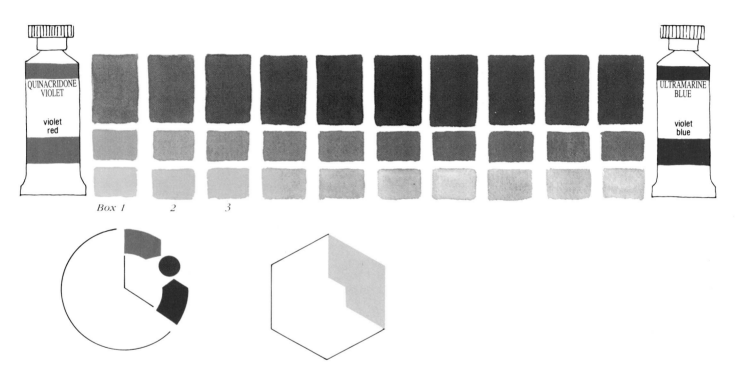

Box 1   2   3

The result is forecast by the colour bias wheel.

This range of violets can be found on colour wheel A, page 54.

Quinacridone Violet and Ultramarine Blue, we know, give a reasonably pure violet - one of the purest of all mixed violets in fact.

In the above exercise, Quinacridone Violet is placed straight from the tube into Box 1. From Box 2 onwards, more Ultramarine is progressively added and the Quinacridone Violet gradually phased out until eventually pure Ultramarine emerges in the final box. Around the mid point is a violet leaning neither towards the blue nor the red.

Each colour has been progressively lightened to form two tints. The watercolourist would normally apply the paint thinly, allowing the whiteness of the paper to provide the tint. The oil or acrylic painter usually adds white paint.

Clear Greens

 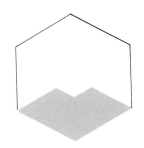

By following the same approach, a range of greens moving from blue-greens to yellow-greens can be created.

This range of greens is found on colour wheel A, page 54.

Clear Oranges

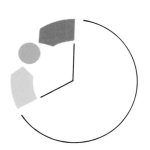 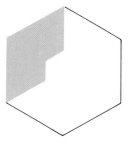

Brighter oranges can be achieved using these two Cadmium colours than are shown here, due to the limitations of conventional colour printing technique.

As mentioned elsewhere in the book, I suggest that you reproduce these exercises yourself in order to gain the maximum benefit.

See colour wheel A on the following page.

Colour Wheel A —
Clear Colours

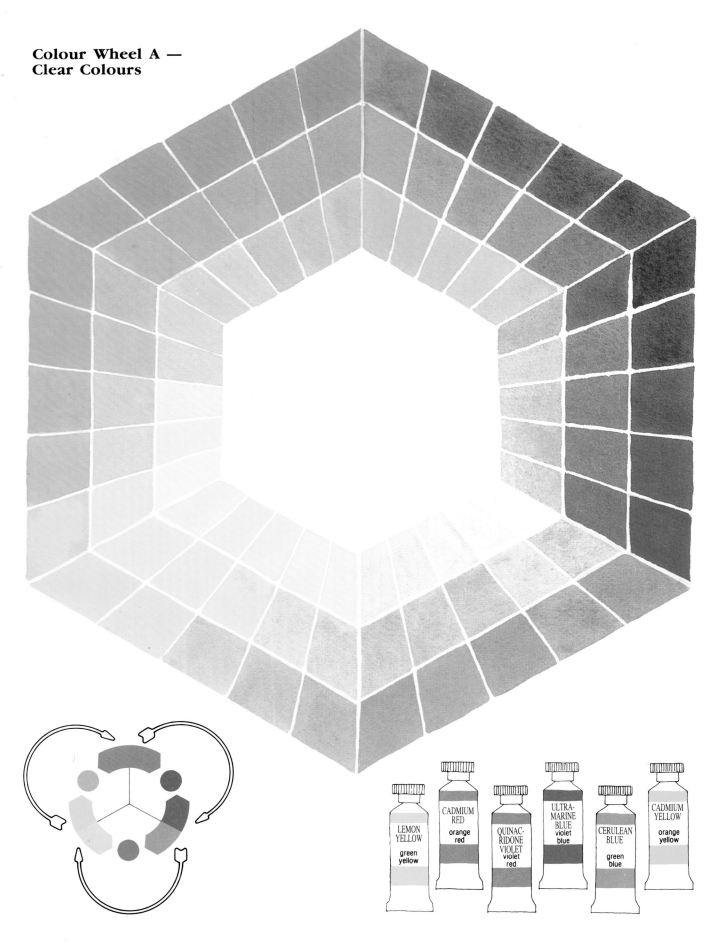

LEMON YELLOW
green yellow

CADMIUM RED
orange red

QUINAC-RIDONE VIOLET
violet red

ULTRA-MARINE BLUE
violet blue

CERULEAN BLUE
green blue

CADMIUM YELLOW
orange yellow

Neutralized Colours

Violets

This type of red points away from the violet position and we can therefore expect dull violets.

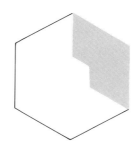

See page 61 for the place of this range on another of the wheels (colour wheel B).

During the initial search for clear violets, greens and oranges we tried contributing colours that proved to be unsuccessful. Cadmium Red and Cerulean Blue, for example, made a very poor violet. But the results were only 'unsuccessful' in as much as they were not clear hues. They are nevertheless interesting and of equal importance to the painter.

Let us turn back and explore the 'unsuccessful' mixes and their tints. The results are recorded on a series of colour wheels (page 61 to 63 which highlight the separate results.

A diagram representing the colour bias wheel is shown with each exercise.

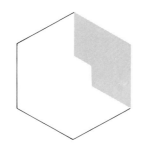

Quinacridone Violet and
Cerulean Blue produce
another quite different series
of dull reds, violets and
blues.

*See Colour Wheel C — page
62.*

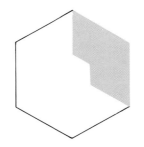

As expected, the dullest
results come from a
combination of Cadmium Red
and Cerulean Blue.

Colour Wheel D — page 63.

Greens

Many paintings look very stilted because the greens lack variation.

Too often artists rely on manufactured, pre-mixed greens which seem to inhibit any desire to mix a wider variety and add interest to the work.

Bear in mind that many of these manufactured green mixes contain poor ingredients, like Chrome Yellow, that fade or change in some other way and eventually spoil the colour.

At this point you are probably able to look at the bias wheel before each exercise and anticipate the 'type' of colour that will emerge from the mixes.

Before

After

Some pre-mixed greens will change with time, others are often simple mixes that you could easily produce yourself.

LEMON YELLOW

green yellow

ULTRAMARINE BLUE

violet blue

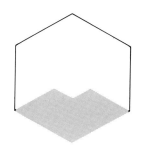

Soft and subdued greens result from a Lemon Yellow/Ultramarine Blue combination.

See Colour wheel B.

Cadmium Yellow Pale and
Cerulean Blue produce slightly
brash greens.

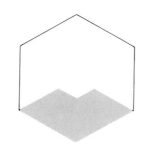

See colour wheel C.

Not surprisingly, two
colours reflecting as little
green as Cadmium Yellow Pale
and Ultramarine Blue produce
some especially greyed or
neutralised greens.

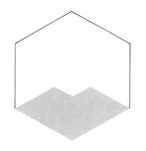

See colour wheel D.

Oranges

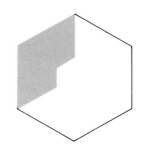

Strong, rather brassy colours are produced from a blend of Cadmium Yellow Pale and Quinacridone Violet.

See colour wheel C.

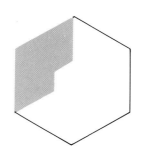

Soft, warmer oranges emerge from Cadmium Red and Lemon Yellow.

See colour wheel B.

Since neither Quinacridone Violet nor Lemon Yellow reflect much orange, they can be expected to produce rather subdued hues.

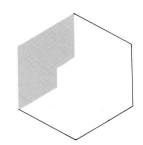

See colour wheel D.

SUMMARY

If we carefully select our contributing paints or inks, we can create clear colours and a wide range of valuable neutralised (dulled) hues.

There are purer, brighter colours available straight from the tube or pan: Cobalt Violet, for example, can be more vivid than the violet mixed from Quinacridone Violet and Ultramarine; Cadmium Orange is usually slightly brighter than any mixed orange, and Phthalocyanine Green or

Viridian are clearer and brighter greens than we can ever mix.

These and other alternatives can certainly have a place, but because they are so bright, many find that they need to be desaturated (dulled), before they can be used.

If you habitually darken, or in some other way modify the brightness of such colours, you are in effect producing hues easily mixed from our limited palette.

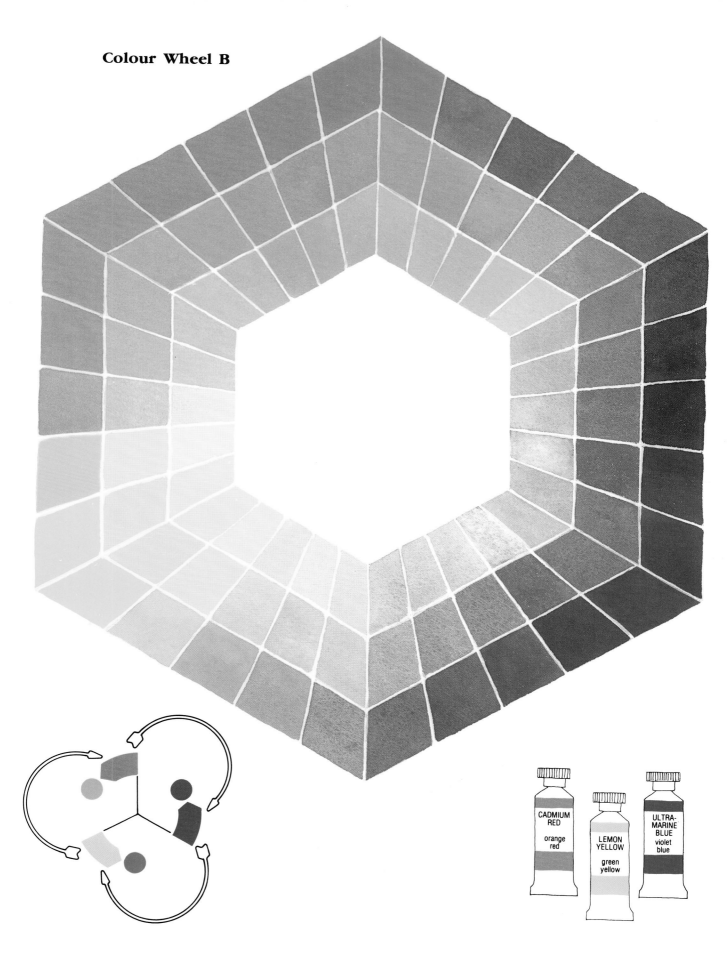

Colour Wheel B

CADMIUM
RED

orange
red

LEMON
YELLOW

green
yellow

ULTRA-
MARINE
BLUE

violet
blue

Colour Wheel C

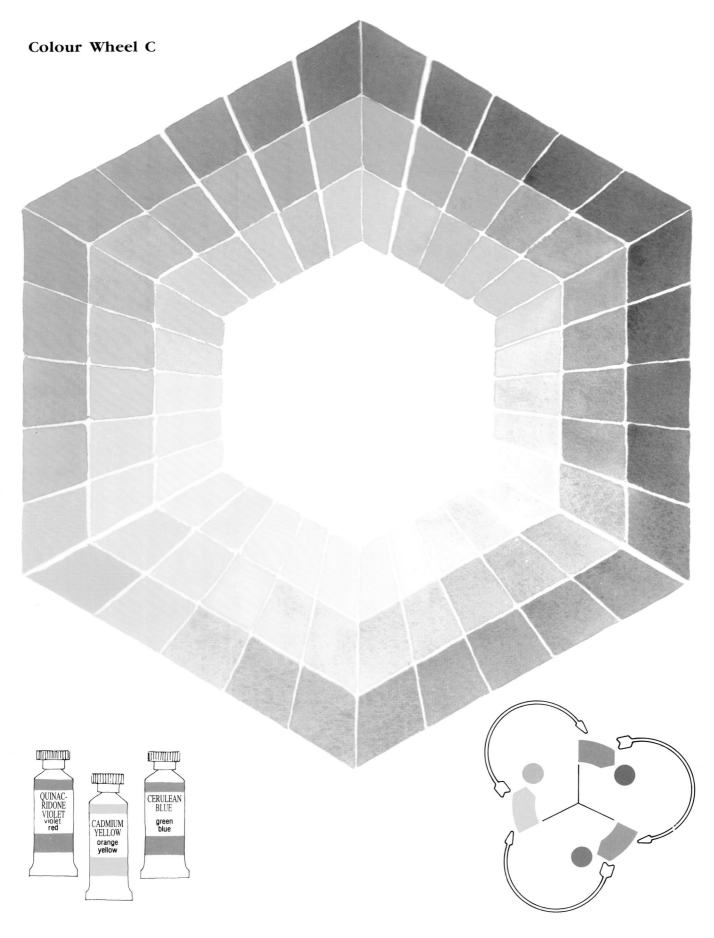

QUINAC-
RIDONE
VIOLET
violet
red

CADMIUM
YELLOW
orange
yellow

CERULEAN
BLUE
green
blue

Colour Wheel D

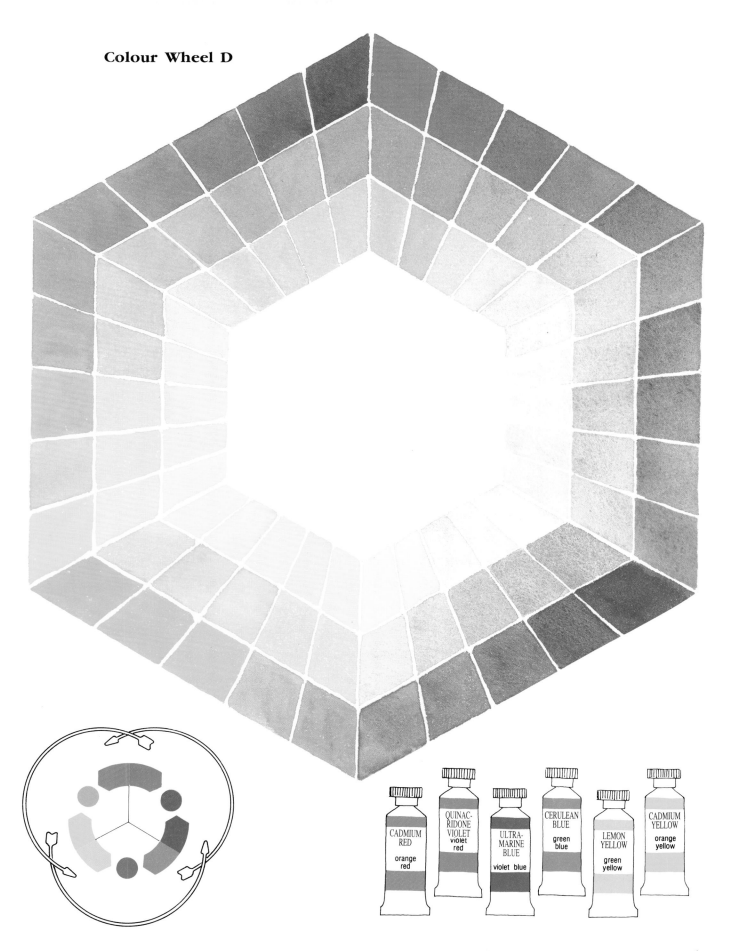

CADMIUM RED	QUINAC-RIDONE VIOLET	ULTRA-MARINE BLUE	CERULEAN BLUE	LEMON YELLOW	CADMIUM YELLOW
orange red	violet red	violet blue	green blue	green yellow	orange yellow

63

Deciding on Colour Type

Reds
Yellows
Blues

Reds

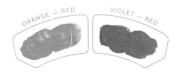

As already mentioned, this approach to colour mixing is based firmly on identifying and using colours according to type. Is a red an orange-red or a violet-red etc.

It is, of course, essential that you are able to identify colours according to their make-up. The various reds available are, for most people, the most difficult to decide upon.

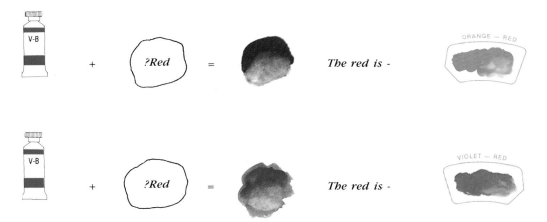

Once you have settled down to a limited palette and have come to associate colour-name with colour-type, (Cadmium Red Light, for example, is an orange-red) it will be smooth sailing until you decide to introduce further colours.

There is a very simple test to decide between the various reds.

Take the red in question and mix it with a known VIOLET-blue, such as Ultramarine Blue.

If the resulting mix is a rather dull, greyed, slightly violet hue, you can be sure that the red in question is an orange-red.

Alternatively, if the result is a bright violet, then, without a doubt, the red has identified itself as being a violet-red.

The results are always as dramatic as these examples. It is a simple test which is foolproof. Of course you need only look back at the section on mixing violets to see exactly why it works.

Yellows

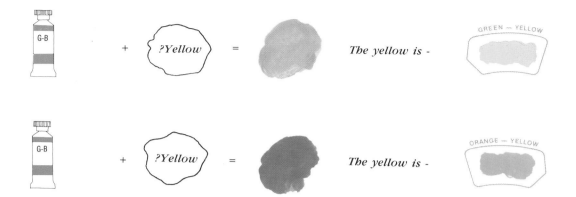

It is usually possible to decide between the various yellows by eye. However, the same type of simple test will quickly confirm the colour-type.

Mix the yellow with a GREEN-blue.

If the yellow happens to be a green-yellow, the result of mixing it with a green blue will be a bright green, as you would expect: green-yellow and green-blue make a bright green.

On the other hand, if the result is a dull, slightly grey green, then the yellow is clearly identified as an orange-yellow. Orange-yellow and green-blue make a mid green.

A good indication of probable colour type with yellows will be the colour-name. Most green-yellows are simply called Lemon Yellow, the majority of other yellows will be orange-yellow.

Blues

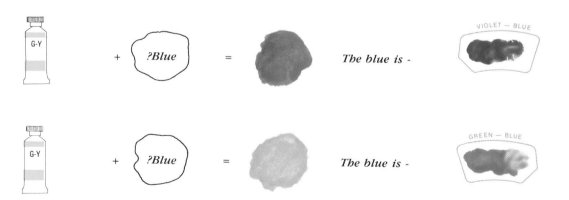

It is very simple to decide on colour-type with blues.

Mix the blue with green-yellow. If you get a slightly dull, mid green then the blue can be identified as violet-blue.

If the mix is a bright green the blue will be a green-blue. Green-yellow and green-blue of course make bright green.

As with yellows, the actual name of a colour will give a good clue as to its type. Ultramarine Blue is the only real violet-blue available, all others can be considered green-blue.

Cobalt Blue is the odd one out. A well made Cobalt Blue will reflect not only blue but a reasonable amount of violet, as well as green. This will allow you to mix reasonable but not particularly bright greens and violets.

As many 'Cobalt Blues' are simply mixes of other, cheaper blues such as Ultramarine and Phthalocyanine Blue, with white, the colour-type will depend on the make up. In every case it is recommended that you try the colour out in a mixing test first.

Greys and Neutral Colours

A colour will set about destroying its complementary partner. We can use this fact to produce subtle neutrals and greys.

Greys and Neutrals from the Complementaries
Yellow/Violet
Blue/Orange
Red/Green
Other Complementary Pairs
Colour Wheel E
Colour Wheel F

Greys and Neutrals from the Complementaries

When red, yellow and blue — traditionally thought of as the painter's 'primaries' — are combined, the subtractive process destroys almost all of the light and the mix begins to move towards black.

If the intensities of the three 'primaries' are all equally balanced, they blend into a very dark grey, approaching black. Remember, the balance refers to intensity and not the actual quantities of paint. Intensity varies from one paint to another.

Greys are darks or non-descript colours that do not have a leaning towards any particular hue.

Neutrals are darkened or dulled hues, such as darkened red or green for example.

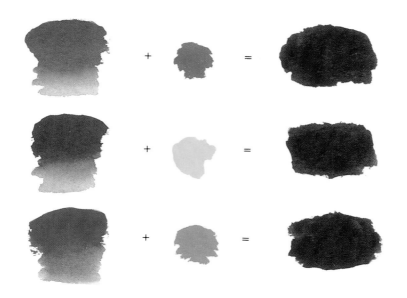

When we were attempting to mix a very dark colour, approaching black, (page 25), we found that if the mix was not quite dark enough we could add another colour to darken it.

If it was rather orange we could introduce a little blue, if violet, yellow, and if it was on the green side, a little red would darken it.

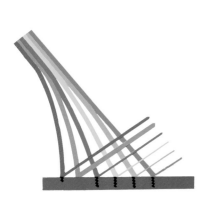

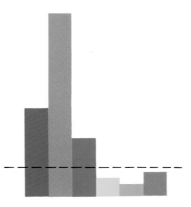

Let's look at the first example — adding blue to orange. We now know that there is no such thing as a pure blue paint. The blues that we use also reflect other colours, most importantly green and violet. Much of the green and violet light will be absorbed by the blue, but enough will escape for us to be able to use this hue as a base colour when mixing either green or violet.

Sufficient blue, green and violet is reflected by any blue pigment to make them important factors to consider when mixing.

But remember the other colours that are also involved: the red, orange and yellow. Tiny amounts of these colours are reflected, while the rest is ABSORBED.

The blue is particularly good at absorbing ORANGE light.

4

3

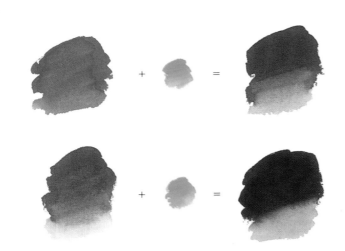

This is why the orange paint was made so much darker when the blue was added. The blue simply set about destroying the orange light before it was able to escape.

For the same reasons, orange paint added to blue destroys the blue light. The orange will reflect a tiny amount of the blue but destroy the remainder.

Blue and orange are therefore mutually destructive. These two colours appear opposite each other on our colour bias wheel, as they do on most colour wheels.

Such colour pairs are known as COMPLEMENTARIES. They are called complementaries for several reasons, one of them being that they mix into a dark grey.

For the same reasons just

outlined, the yellow destroys the violet and the red the green in the examples, page 67.

Yellow/violet and red/green are also complementary pairs.

We can use the fact that a colour will set about destroying its complementary partner to produce some very interesting and subtle colours.

Yellow/Violet

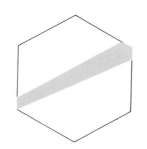

See Colour Wheel E — page 73.

Pure Cadmium Yellow Pale is used in box (1), to which a touch of the violet is added to produce box (2). By adding more and more violet the colour is taken through a series of neutralised yellows, through a coloured grey and a range of neutral violets before finally emerging in clear violet. Tints are made in the usual way. Notice how dark the middle colours become when the subtraction of light is at its greatest. The red, yellow and blue are really attacking each other with gusto!

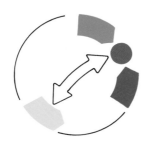

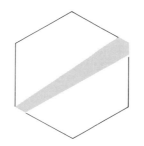

Colour Wheel E — page 73.

The second exercise calls for mixing Lemon Yellow with the violet. Note the subtle difference in results produced by the two types of yellow.

Blue/Orange

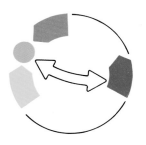

Blue and orange produce another grey when they approach equal intensities.

In this exercise, Ultramarine Blue is progressively added to a mixed orange (Cadmium Red and Cadmium Yellow Pale).

Colour Wheel E — page 73.

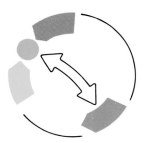

The blue is changed to Cerulean in the second exercise and the differences, although slight, are definitely apparent.

As expected, the Cerulean Blue adds a certain amount of green while the Ultramarine Blue exerts a violet influence.

Colour Wheel E — page 73.

Red/Green

Colour Wheel E

The darks produced from a mix of Quinacridone Violet and green become particularly subtle when lightened.

The Cadmium Red gives a markedly warmer mix due to its orange bias which is in contrast to the cool, violet influence of the Quinacridone Violet.

Nature's range of greens seems almost limitless yet so many painters appear to close their eyes to this profuse

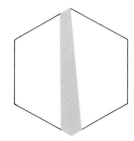

Colour Wheel E

variety and use just two or three greens in any one piece of work.

These greens are usually very straightforward mixes of blue and yellow or else come directly from the tube.

Adding a little red very often gives a more authentic result - it is certainly the ideal way to neutralize or dull any green. In return, green subdues a red very satisfactorily.

Other Complementary Pairs

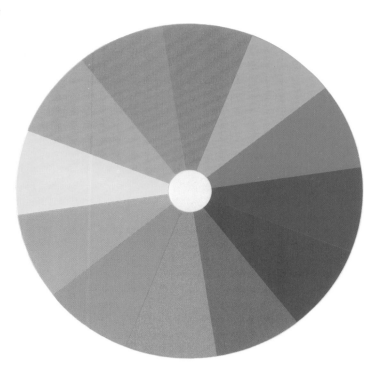

Any complementary pair can be mixed to produce a range of both neutral colours and greys. Shown here are just a few of the possible combinations.

Complementaries can be found opposite each other on many types of artist's colour wheel.

An ideal way to create a shade is to add a touch of the colour's complementary, rather than adding black. The neutralized colours and greys in this series of exercises — usually described as 'muddy' and discarded — can be used to great effect to accentuate smaller areas of bright, complementary colour.

A greyed-blue with touches of clean orange is one example. These colours are extremely important when we are seeking contrast or harmony.

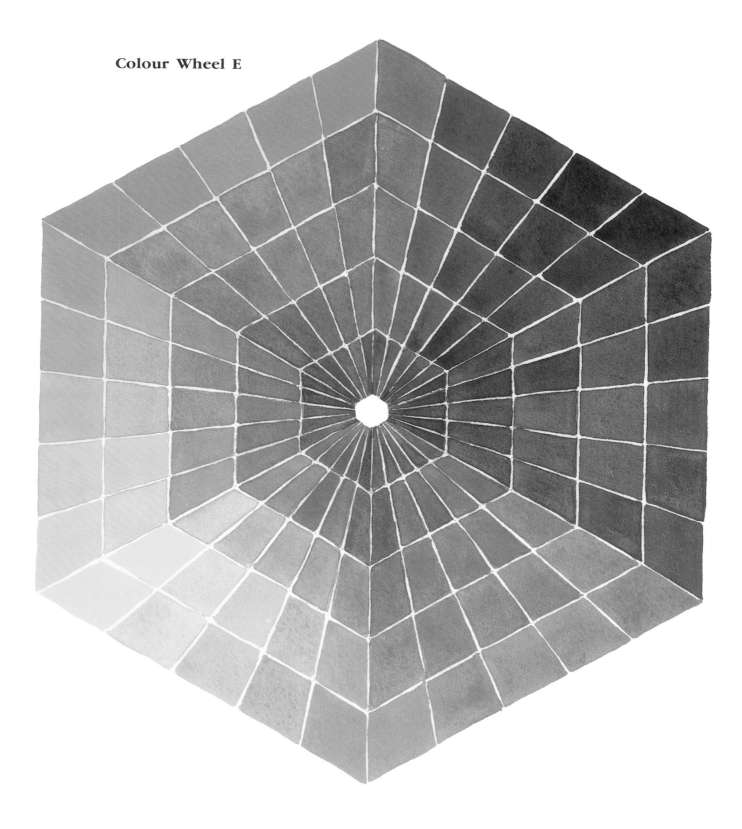

Colour Wheel E

In this wheel, the exercises
on mixing complementaries
have all been brought together
to show their relevant
positions and to emphasize the
profusion of neutrals and greys
that can be achieved.

Colour Wheel F

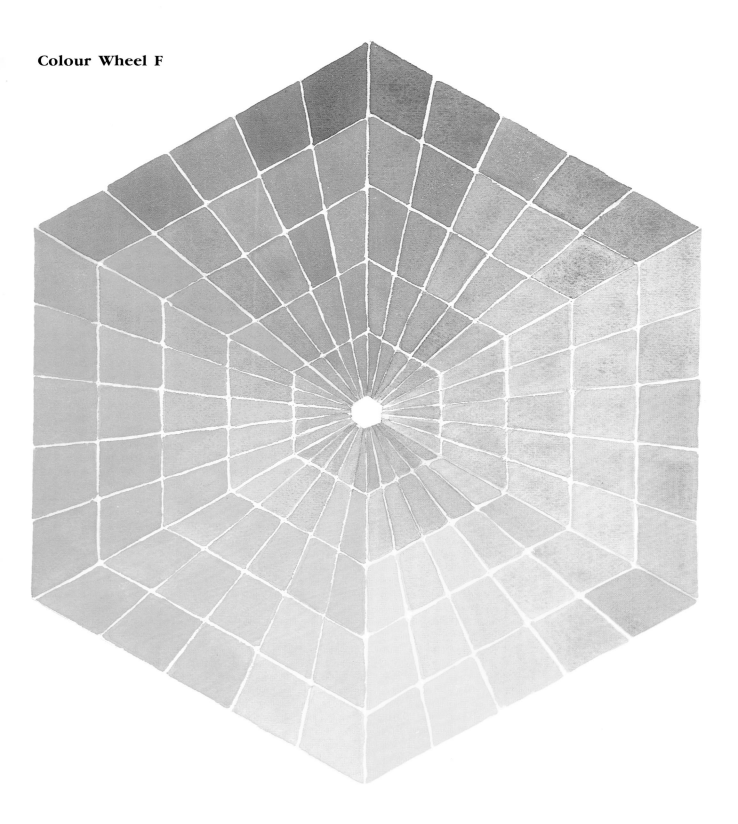

To avoid confusion the tints of these mixes have been recorded on a separate wheel.

You can easily duplicate these exercises and with practice you will be able to select a colour and take it in whichever direction you choose. Try and form a mental picture as you are mixing the colours of just what is taking place inside the paint film: why, for instance, does one blue take orange towards green while the other does not? Think through each exercise, work out why certain colours or 'types' of colour emerge. By making notes of your observations you will gradually come to understand and control your colour mixing.

Transparent, Semi-Transparent and Opaque Paints

The essential differences in opacity between paints is often overlooked — yet such differences are of vital importance.

Paint Films
Transparent Colours
Colour Wheel G
Further Transparent Colours

Opaque Colours
Colour Wheel H
Further Opaque Colours

Paint Films

Certain colours are prized for their transparency while others are valued for their opacity. These qualities are dependent upon the careful preparation and selection of the pigments used during manufacture.

Transparent paints and inks allow underlying colours to influence the final result and in particular make it possible to create tints through their application over a white ground.

The more opaque colours are ideal for covering previous work, showing detail and adding 'body' to a piece of work.

Unfortunately many painters overlook these qualities and use transparent, semi-transparent and opaque paints as if they were all the same. Typically they attempt to cover earlier work with transparent colours or lose subtle effects through the over enthusiastic use of more opaque colours.

A carefully planned combination of opaque, semi-transparent and transparent colours in a painting creates an emphasis between the heavier opaque colours and the vibrant transparent passages.

An entirely opaque painting often looks dull and heavy while a completely transparent piece can appear 'washed out'. The mixes produced so far are a combination of varying degrees of opacity.

The Opaque Paint Film

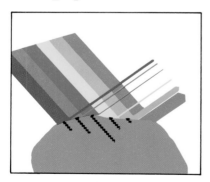

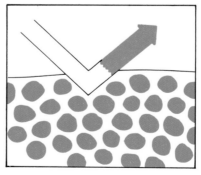

All the paint film diagrams depicted so far represent opaque paint films where the subtraction or reflection of light takes place very close to the surface of the pigment particle.

The particles of opaque pigment within the paint film prevent the light penetrating.

The Transparent Paint Film

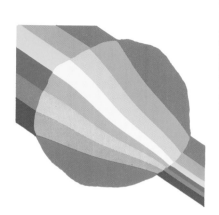

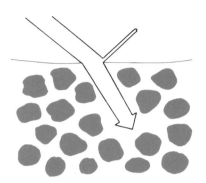

The pigment particle in transparent paint, on the other hand, allows light to travel through it without difficulty; subtraction takes place within the particle rather than close to the surface.

With two or more transparent colours, the subtractive process takes place in the same way as opaque pigments but within the particles rather than close to their surfaces.

Because light passes so easily through the pigment, much of it sinks well into the paint film.

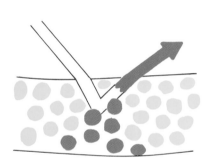

Thinly applied transparent paint will allow the light to pass easily through it and pick up any colour underneath.

Such colours are taken back to the surface of the paint and become visible.

A thickly applied layer of transparent paint allows the light to sink in deeply where its energy is dissipated and only a little is able to struggle back to the surface. The result can be a dark, almost black colour.

Semi-Transparent Paint Films

By comparison with transparent pigment, semi-transparent pigment allows a smaller proportion of light to enter and reflects the rest.

Transparent Colours

Transparency Test

It is a simple matter to decide on the transparency of a particular colour.

Apply a uniformly thick layer of paint over a black line (which should be insoluble). If the line disappears the paint is obviously opaque; semi-transparent paint will partly obliterate the line, and if the line shows clearly it indicates an especially clear paint.

The test illustrated here shows that Light Red, Cerulean and Cadmium Red are opaque, Cadmium Yellow semi-transparent and the others transparent.

In order to increase the range of transparent hues we need to introduce several new colours to the palette.

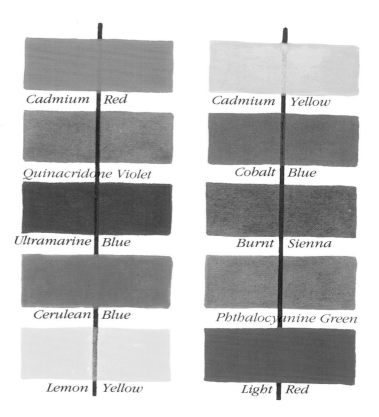

Cadmium Red

Quinacridone Violet

Ultramarine Blue

Cerulean Blue

Lemon Yellow

Cadmium Yellow

Cobalt Blue

Burnt Sienna

Phthalocyanine Green

Light Red

Phthalocyanine Green
Pigment Green 7 or 36

This is a colour which must be handled with some care due to its rather strong tinting power. Being particularly transparent and almost iridescent, it is highly valued as a glazing colour

A very clear, cool, strong green which will only reveal its true beauty when applied thinly. Unfortunately it is often applied heavily, when it takes on a dull, almost blackish appearance.

It seems almost a waste to apply such colours without care. Particularly as earlier artists would have given almost anything for the incredible range at our disposal.

They would have valued such colours as this for their very transparency and not have applied them with a heavy hand.

For landscape painting in particular, a wide choice of clear, vibrant greens is essential. Phthalocyanine Green can form a base for such colours.

It is a close cousin of Viridian as far as colour and transparency are concerned.

Cobalt Blue
Pigment Blue 28

A popular blue and a standard for many artists. The transparency tends to vary depending on manufacturer.

A well produced Cobalt Blue can be reasonably transparent. The bias of this colour tends to vary, leaning either towards violet or green.

Burnt Sienna
Pigment Brown 7

A well produced Burnt Sienna is a brilliant, fiery, rich red to orange brown.

It makes an excellent glazing colour because of its transparency.

Applied in a thin layer for glazing purposes, Burnt Sienna displays its true beauty.

Because it does not have a strong bias in either direction it is often erroneously described as being a pure blue. A rather weak colour in mixes, it is easily swamped.

This is the least chalky of the red-browns and can add great depth and clarity to many mixes, especially when combined with other transparent colours. For colour mixing purposes it is best described as a neutralized orange.

Transparent Greens

It is vital to experiment with all new colours to discover their characteristics, colour bias and transparency.

The opacity of Cerulean Blue will tend to make the blue greens semi opaque. This influence will diminish over the range and the mid greens will be reasonably transparent.

The results given by these two colours will be very dependant on the make of the Cobalt Blue.

A reasonably transparent example will give fresh, clear blue-greens. Cobalt Blue is a better choice than Cerulean

when transparency is sought (though less so when 'body' is required).

In this exercise we still find clear blue-greens but they are slightly neutralized due to the violet content of the Ultramarine Blue.

The properties of the three blues - Cerulean, Ultramarine and Cobalt - will become more apparent with experience.

Phthalocyanine Blue is also worth experimenting with. It is a vibrant, very transparent green-blue.

You will need to use a quality Lemon Yellow to obtain transparent results. Cheaper varieties can be very

chalky due to an excess of filler.

It is always worth choosing your colours with care. When

you have control of colour mixing and no longer waste materials, it will pay you to use only the very best.

A Phthalocyanine Green and Cadmium Yellow mix gives a variety of reasonably transparent yellow-greens when applied thinly.

Such greens are noticeably different in character to the Lemon Yellow/Phthalo Green mixes shown on the previous page.

A well made Cadmium Yellow, although an opaque colour, has sufficient strength to be used in thin layers and appear transparent.

Delicate, reasonably transparent greens are made from a mix of Lemon Yellow and Cobalt Blue

Any of the transparent greens can be dulled or neutralized simply by adding the complementary red. It is not necessary for mixing purposes to exactly match up complementaries; any red will move any green towards grey. Varying the reds or greens used will give differing results, but the principles of subtractive colour mixing apply, whatever the pairing.

Quinacridone Violet is very transparent and therefore makes a good choice of red in this exercise.

It is also, incidentally, close to the true complementary of Phthalocyanine Green.

This exercise illustrates the ability of Phthalocyanine Green and Quinacridone Violet to soften each other's abrasiveness and lessen their tendency to clash with other colours.

Neutralized hues like these come into their own when colour harmony is sought.

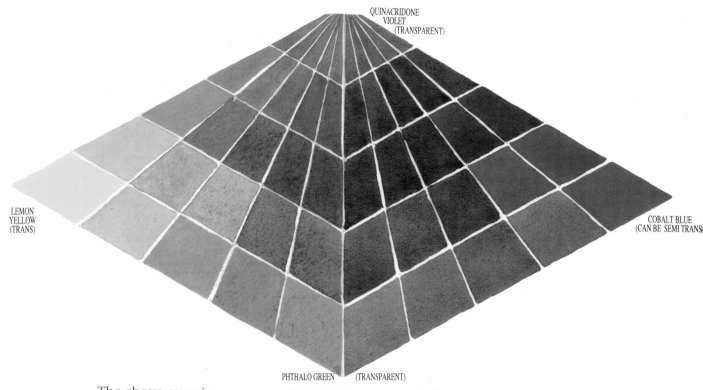

QUINACRIDONE
VIOLET
(TRANSPARENT)

LEMON
YELLOW
(TRANS)

COBALT BLUE
(CAN BE SEMI TRANS)

PHTHALO GREEN   (TRANSPARENT)

The above exercise explores the range of neutralized colours derived from mixing Quinacridone Violet with a series of transparent greens. It also demonstrates that exact complementaries need not be chosen to neutralize a colour. These soft, transparent hues begin to demonstrate the enormous variety of available colours provided by even a limited palette.

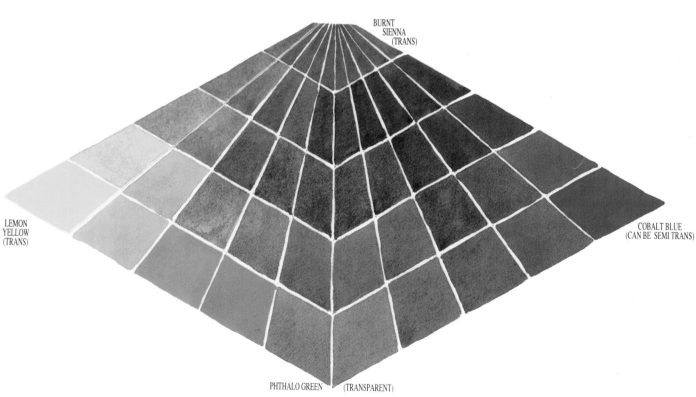

BURNT
SIENNA
(TRANS)

LEMON
YELLOW
(TRANS)

COBALT BLUE
(CAN BE SEMI TRANS)

PHTHALO GREEN   (TRANSPARENT)

Those greens not in a near complementary relationship with Quinacridone Violet or Burnt Sienna still mix into useful colours, but they are more difficult to forecast.

Transparent Violets

Quinacridone Violet and Ultramarine Blue, as we have seen already, form one of the purest, mixed transparent violets.

Another useful series of violets, this time slightly less intense, can be mixed from Cobalt Blue and Quinacridone Violet.

As Cobalt Blue reflects violet less effectively than Ultramarine, the results will be a little more subdued as less violet will be left behind.

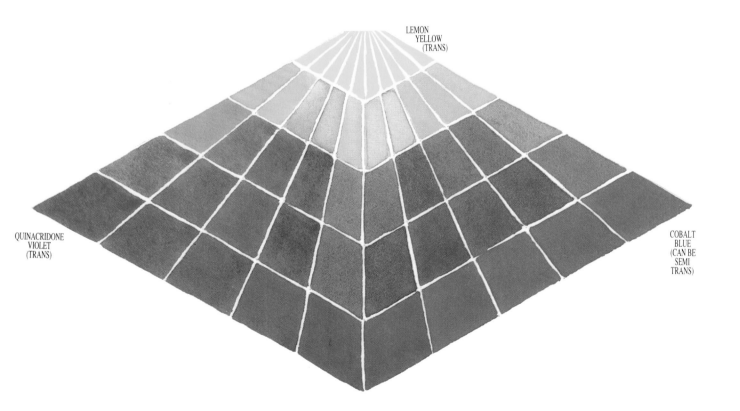

The softening effect of the Lemon Yellow is most apparent with the violet segment and dissipates as it approaches the red and blue positions.

Transparent Oranges

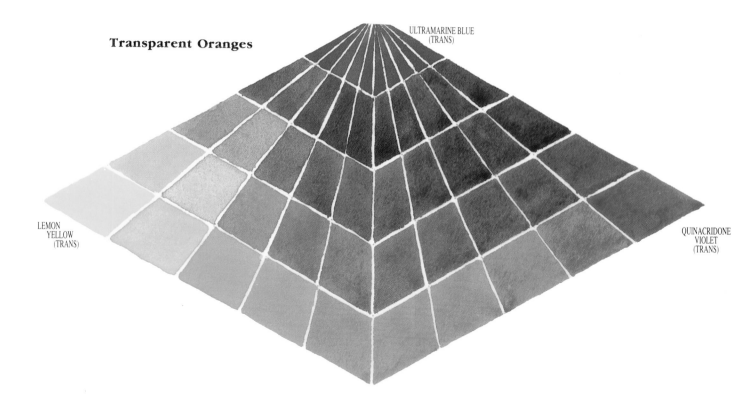

LEMON
YELLOW
(TRANS)

ULTRAMARINE BLUE
(TRANS)

QUINACRIDONE
VIOLET
(TRANS)

Strong, clear oranges can be difficult to place harmoniously within a piece of work.

Although they certainly have a place in the colourists repertoire, their use is often regarded as rather limited.

Accordingly, we will concentrate only on the more subdued oranges.

The neutralized oranges mixed from Quinacridone Violet and Lemon Yellow are effectively cooled and further dulled by adding blue.

Note the greying effects of the orange on the blue.

PURE TRANSPARENT ORANGES

Pure transparent oranges can be obtained but it means adding further colours, which have the following drawbacks:

1. The clearest orange-yellows and orange-reds are often powerful colours that combine to produce oranges many painters find too bright for transparent colour work.

2. Such colours are often prone to fading and can be very expensive.

It is an easy matter to add these hues to your palette and some simple tests will show their colour bias and transparency. But take care that the colours you select are lightfast because paint applied in very thin layers can be prone to fading.

Colour Wheel G

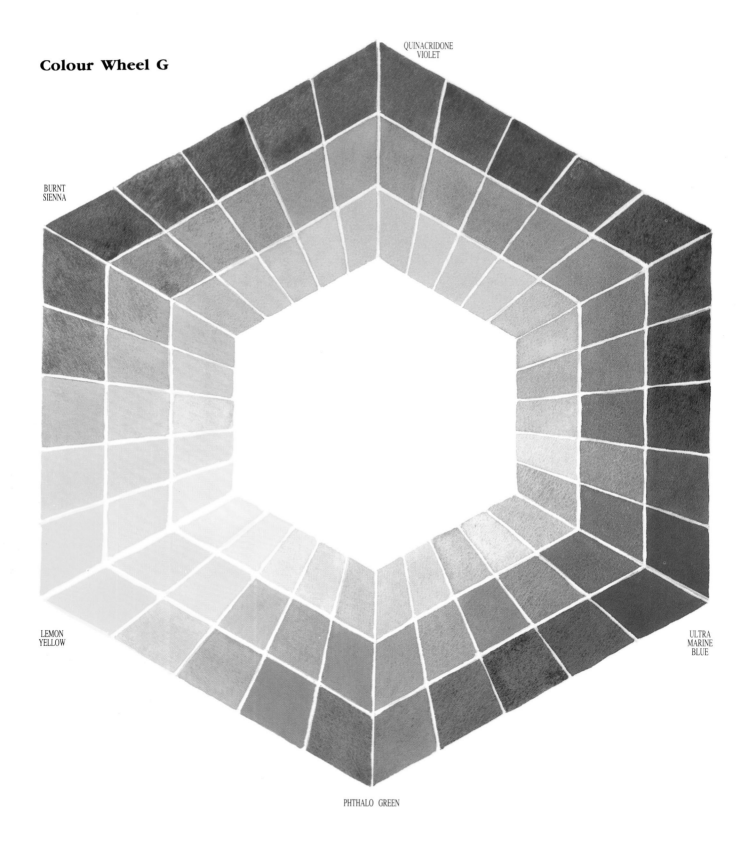

QUINACRIDONE
VIOLET

BURNT
SIENNA

LEMON
YELLOW

ULTRA
MARINE
BLUE

PHTHALO GREEN

This wheel of transparent colours illustrates just one potential combination. It can be varied by, for example, removing the Burnt Sienna (for a different series of neutral oranges), or by taking out the Phthalo Green to give other transparent greens.

Alternatively, further clear colours can be introduced replacing those used here.

84

Further Transparent Colours

Other suitable transparent colours include:

Quinacridone Reds

Usually sold under a variety of trade names and vague, fancy titles such as Geranium, Rose or Scarlet.

There are several types of Quinacridone compound on the market which give a wide range of exceptionally transparent reds. These clean, brilliant reds invariably have a slightly violet bias making them less suitable for mixing clear oranges.

Particularly clear and lightfast are:-

Quinacridone Magenta —
Pigment Red 122
Quinacridone Red —
Pigment Red 192
Quinacridone Scarlet —
Pigment Red 207

Phthalocyanine Blue
Pigment Blue 15

Also sold under a variety of exotic titles and names. An extremely powerful, vibrant, deep greenish-blue that must be used cautiously due to its high strength. Lightfast, inexpensive and very transparent.

Varidian
Pigment Green 18

Viridian is very similar in both colour and transparency to Phthalocyanine Green.
Both are very transparent and rather strong colours.
A clean, powerful colour that can dominate others if used without care.
As with Phthalo Green, it is darkened very effectively by adding Quinacridone Violet, is close complementary.

Aureolin or Cobalt Yellow
Pigment Yellow 40

Sold under both names, Aureolin is a very bright, transparent colour which, applied thinly, approaches a pure yellow. While prized for its transparency this colour does possess a fair degree of covering power and a quite strong tinting strength. Aureolin takes on a very dull appearance if it is applied heavily as a body colour.

Carefully manufactured, it is relatively lightfast (xxx) but some manufacturers give their product a lower lightfastness rating (xx) so choose carefully.

There is an extensive choice of transparent colours on the market which vary in permanency and value for money. Be very careful. Check the resistance to light very thoroughly and preferably try to restrict your palette to a range of colours over which you will have full control. The fewer the better in most cases.

Opaque Colours

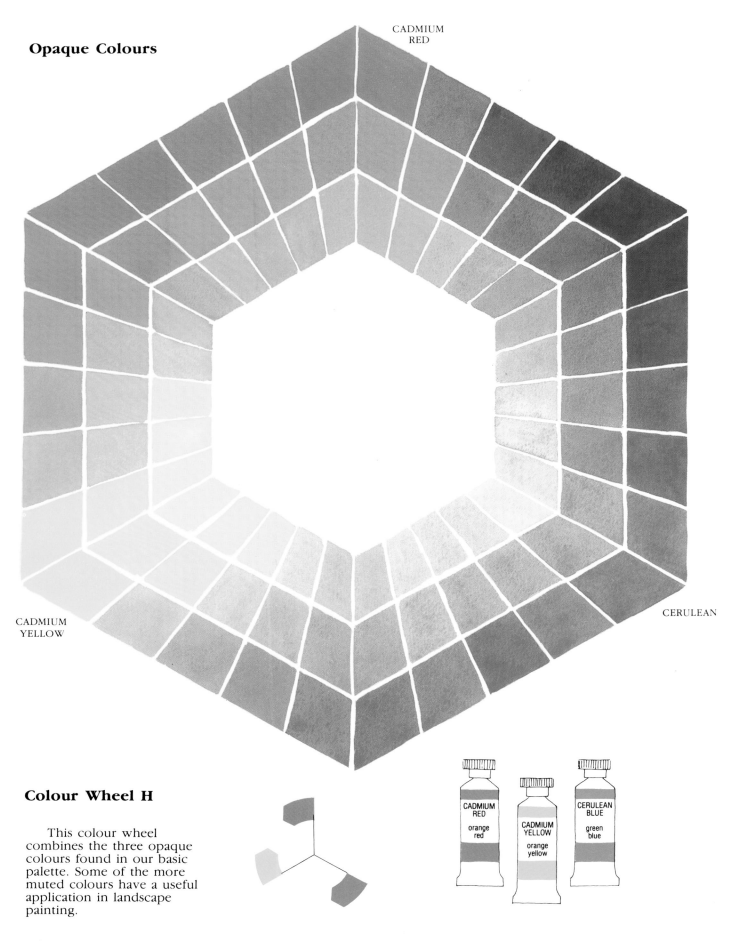

CADMIUM
RED

CADMIUM
YELLOW

CERULEAN

Colour Wheel H

This colour wheel combines the three opaque colours found in our basic palette. Some of the more muted colours have a useful application in landscape painting.

CADMIUM
RED

orange
red

CADMIUM
YELLOW

orange
yellow

CERULEAN
BLUE

green
blue

86

Further Opaque Colours

Light Red Oxide
Pigment Red 101

Two other opaque colours worth considering are Yellow Ochre and Light Red.

Yellow Ochre
Pigment Yellow 40

A soft, golden yellow that works and mixes well and brings a certain calm to other colours. Good quality makes are fairly transparent in thin layers but Yellow Ochre can generally be considered opaque.

It is extremely reliable because of its lightfastness.

Also called English Red Oxide, English Red and Light Red.

Opaque, with good tinting strength, the colour varies considerably from one manufacturer to another, so check all available brands.

Mixed with white or used as a wash, a range of very attractive, subtle salmon pinks emerge. As with many colours, this undertone or undercolour is often overlooked. Many consider such undertones to be more beautiful than the mass tone or top colour.

Equally reliable alternatives are Mars Red and Indian Red.

Yellow Ochre can bring calm to other colours.

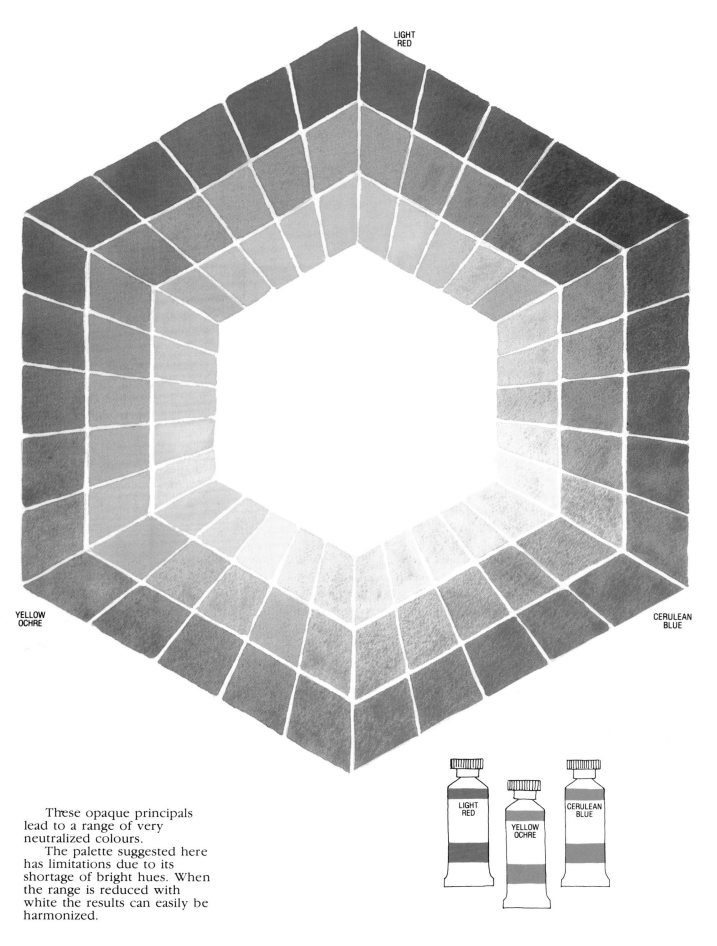

LIGHT
RED

YELLOW
OCHRE

CERULEAN
BLUE

LIGHT
RED

YELLOW
OCHRE

CERULEAN
BLUE

These opaque principals lead to a range of very neutralized colours.

The palette suggested here has limitations due to its shortage of bright hues. When the range is reduced with white the results can easily be harmonized.

Adding White and Black

Colours are cooled and brilliance is damaged by the addition of white, yet its use is often essential.

The debate over whether or not black should be included in the palette continues, with strong feelings being expressed by both camps.

Adding White
Adding Black

Mixed with white   As a wash

Mixed with white   As a wash

Mixed with white   As a wash

Mixed with white   As a wash

Mixed with white   As a wash

Mixed with white   As a wash

Tints can be produced by either adding white paint or allowing the white painting surface to show through by applying the colour thinly.

Colour brilliance is damaged by adding white paint and this is particularly noticeable in watercolour painting, which relies heavily on clean, transparent tints for much of its effect.

The second method gives the clearest, brightest tints.

Oil and acrylic painters, who usually add white paint to lighten colours, should not overlook the possibility of allowing white underpainting, or white priming, to lighten thinly applied top layers.

In every medium, brilliance is lost and colours are cooled by adding white paint. The warmer colours in particular are cooled by white.

The blues, already cool, suffer less than other colours and retain their character reasonably well.

If need be, steps can sometimes be taken to counteract the cooling effect of the white. A touch of a warm colour can 'boost' the temperature.

An excellent example is violet. When it is reduced to a tint by being applied thinly, violet stays close in temperature and character to the saturated colour.

The same violet however, mixed wi white paint, taken on a different character and is dramatically cooled. Just by adding a little Quinacridone Violet to the violet tint, we can counteract the white paint's cooling influence.

Plus a little Quinacridone violet

Plus a little Quinacridone violet

As a wash.

Mixed with white.

White paints vary markedly in their characteristics and suitability and should be chosen carefully.

Flake White or White Lead
Pigment White 1

In use as a pigment since oil painting began, White Lead has more than proved its worth. Paintings hundreds of years old containing areas in this extraordinary pigment have remained intact while the rest of the work has long since deteriorated.

Due to its chemical reaction with drying oils, Flake White forms an extremely durable and flexible paint film. These qualities, together with its opacity, quick drying capability and buttery texture set it well apart from other pigments.

The drawbacks associated with this white are often exaggerated. True it darkens if exposed to Hydrogen Sulphide in the atmosphere, which makes it unsuitable for use as a watercolour, but made up into an oil paint, it is easily protected by a layer of varnish.

Problems can occur when Flake White is mixed with certain low-grade pigment, especially poorly made Cadmium colours, Vermilion and Cobalt Violet.

No such difficulties arise with high quality pigments which the discerning artist will always use. Flake White can usually only be obtained in oil or alkyd paint.

Flake White is a warm and creamy white, qualities that it imparts to mixes.

Titanium White
Pigment White 6

This relatively modern white has removed the concerns associated with combining Flake White and certain poorly produced colours.

Titanium White is a useful covering paint, either alone or in mixes. Its use renders paint films opaque.

This white is absolutely inert, being unaffected by other pigments, light, heat, weak acids or alkaline. Generally considered to be absolutely permanent.

Although an excellent white, it has not replaced Flake White or Zinc Oxide as it has neither the warmth of the former in mixes nor the transparency of the latter. It is not quite as pleasant to use as Flake White since it lacks the buttery texture of that paint. Titanium White is usually only found in oil, acrylic and alkyd paints, although it is also suitable for watercolours.

Titanium White is a lot cooler in mixes than Flake White. It is extremely brilliant and the whitest of the whites.

 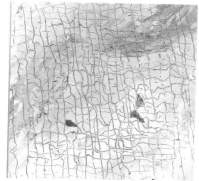

Zinc White
Pigment White 4

A very permanent white that is perfectly safe to use with all other pigments. It is a very pure, cold white. Used in oil paints, it tends to dry to a brittle film which is very prone to cracking. One of the most transparent of the whites.

Zinc White is often used for glazing purposes, either alone or in mixes with other transparent colours. Unless you particularly wish to use a white for glazing, this is a poor buy as an oil paint because the hard, brittle film it forms represents a major defect. Whereas Flake White has lasted very well on many old paintings, Zinc White has often led to the rapid deterioration of the work.

Chinese White

The watercolour Chinese White is a specially prepared, very dense type of Zinc Oxide with a greater covering power than the oil version.

It is the principal white of the watercolourist. Beware of cheaper grades labelled Chinese White as they are often ordinary Zinc White.

There should be little call for using a white in watercolour painting because the paper itself provides the whites and tints.

The Watercolour painter has little need for white paint, it both cools and dulls other colours.

Adding Black

A black surface effectively absorbs almost all light striking it due to its molecular make-up. Added to another colour, black pigment absorbs nearly all the light reflected from that other colour.

A black paint absorbs light very efficiently and takes on a darker appearance than a mixed dark.

The debate over whether or not black should be included in the palette continues, with strong feelings expressed by both camps.

Those favouring the use of black argue that black paint must be used to depict extremely dark areas accurately. Another view put forward is that black is a very convenient way to darken a colour.

Let us examine these two arguments:

1. BLACK PAINT MUST BE USED TO DEPICT VERY DARK AREAS.

On the surface this appears plausible.

However, most areas deprived of light are closer to dark grey than black and in fact pure black itself is seldom found in nature.

Many 'blacks' such as say, animal fur, bird feathers and fruits are, on closer inspection, seething with subdued colour. Depicted with black paint they take on a dead appearance.

Trees and other similar objects silhouetted against an evening sky look heavy and unnatural if painted black. The reality is that such darkness is never a true black.

A mixed dark always looks far more natural, containing, as it does, some of the light that will be present on such an evening.

Even the interior of an unlit room in the dead of night does not look entirely black but a deep, shifting, atmospheric dark grey.

If we shut our eyes in total darkness, we do not experience a sensation of total blackness — faint lights seem to wander around in front of our eyes.

There is even a danger in depicting naturally occurring blacks with black paint.

If, for instance, a burnt tree stump is depicted with black, it seldom looks realistic because the effect of distance tends to blur detail and soften the black into a dark grey.

Were the painter to use pure black in depicting this tree, the viewer would be confronted with a black that is too sharp and dense to be realistic.

Perhaps the strongest argument against its use to portray dark areas is that the final result often looks more like a hole in the painting surface than part of the work.

There is a distinct possibility that you will depict damage to your painting rather than portray areas of dark, should you decide to use black unmodified by other colours.

2. BLACK IS A CONVENIENT WAY TO DARKEN A COLOUR.

The addition of black to a hue gives widely varying results:

It moves violet, the darkest of the hues, towards a shade with little damage to its character; blue quickly loses its brilliance; reds are changed in character, although some interesting colours can be obtained; blue-green takes to black rather well, yellow-green less so; and yellow is damaged out of all recognition by even tiny amounts of black and moves quickly towards a series of greens that many find unwholesome.

There is no such thing as an 'incorrect' colour and indeed some useful results can be obtained by using black. It has to be said, however, that many, including the author, find that black has the effect of 'dirtying' colours to such an extent that its use is seldom if ever considered.

If we combine a colour with its complementary, or mix red, yellow and blue together, we can readily and accurately depict the darks found in nature.

Black often upsets the balance of otherwise harmonious arrangements. What better way to darken a colour can there be than to add its complementary?

Yet, with all that in mind, the use of black must remain an individual decision.

Lamp Black
Pigment Black 6

Ivory Black
Pigment Black 9

Mars Black
Pigment Black 11

Soot given off from the fire was probably the first pigment ever to be used. Lamp Black, produced by burning a wide range of materials, has been in constant use since the cave painter.

Lamp black is a cool, bluish black which varies from transparent to semi-transparent. Quite high in tinting strength, with excellent covering power. It is a slow drier in oils.

Raw Umber is often added by the oil painter in order to speed up the drying rate.

When used in water colour and applied in a very wet layer, the pigment is apt to float to the top of the film and separate from other colours. Not usually available as an acrylic.

Value for money if you require a permanent blue-black.

Most black pigments are still produced from carbon obtained by burning various materials such as oils, tars and animal or vegetable matter.

Originally made by charring ivory scraps in sealed crucibles, it was sold side by side with an inferior black made from charred animal bones, Bone Black.

When the supply of ivory dried up the paint manufacturers found themselves in a quandry. Ivory Black had gained a favourable reputation among painters and it seemed a shame to take it off the market. The answer was to rename the less favourable Bone Black as Ivory Black.

Today Bone Black still remains with us, masquerading as Ivory Black.

It varies from semi-transparent to opaque, with reasonably good covering power. The colour of the product has changed over recent years. Normally possessing a warm brown undertone, manufacturers now strive to produce a darker, almost blue black. Prussian Blue is often added in order to darken the colour.

An artificial mineral pigment, Mars Black is a recent addition to the artists' palette. Dense and reliable, the better qualities have been generally welcomed by today's painter.

A deep, warm, brownish black with fairly good tinting strength and very good covering qualities.

In oils it is an average drier, but certainly quicker than Ivory Black.

Suitable for water colour although not generally available.

Being more inert than the carbon blacks, Mars black is especially suitable for acrylic and PVC emulsions.

The better qualities are value for money.

Browns

*Certain browns are invaluable, but many
can easily be mixed from our limited palette.*

How to Make your own Browns
Manufactured Browns

How to Make your own Browns

Artists needing a brown
invariably reach for a
manufactured colour, yet a
wide range of browns can
very easily be mixed from our
limited palette.

Asked to identify their idea
of brown, painters invariably
select from amongst a range of
darkened yellows, oranges and
reds.

We now know that the

ideal way to darken such
colours is to add a touch of
their complementary, for
example violet into yellow,
blue into orange and green
into red.

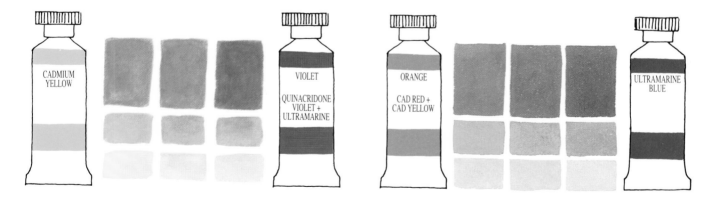

Manufactured Browns

As you will gather from the exercises, an extensive range of browns can be easily mixed. Most are simply darkened yellows, oranges and reds. You might, however, find the following prepared browns of value.

Raw Umber
Pigment Brown 7

Similar in make-up to Raw Sienna, hence the same Colour Index Number. A particularly pleasant, cool, dark, slightly greenish brown (in the better qualities). Some grades are fairly transparent when applied in thin layers. The products of different manufacturers can vary widely in colour. Lightfast and compatible with other pigments, it is considered a must by many painters.

Burnt Umber
Pigment Brown 7

A warm, rich, fairly 'heavy' orange-brown prepared by roasting Raw Umber.

Extremely lightfast and compatible with all other pigments it is a valuable and versatile brown, considered as an essential by many. Suitable for all media.

Close matches can be mixed but they invariably require the addition of black, which tends to give a less pleasant colour.

When mixed with a blue such as Ultramarine it will give rich, deep powerful darks which many consider to be superior to any black paint. The result is so dark because in effect Burnt Umber can be considered a neutral orange and combined with blue we obtain a mix of complementaries.

Raw Sienna
Pigment Brown 7

Absolutely lightfast and compatible with all other pigments, Raw Sienna lies between Yellow Ochre and Burnt Sienna in colour.

Being very transparent, Raw Sienna is an excellent glazing colour — a quality that is seldom made use of. It is possible to obtain a similar colour through mixing, but not one of such transparency.

Raw Sienna has a place on most artists' palettes. It is unsurpassed by modern synthetic products (such as Mars Brown) for beauty, luminosity and permanence.

Other Browns

Other browns can have a place on the palette, but be careful in their selection.

Mars Brown

Van Dyke Brown

Sepia

Mars Brown can be useful, but is harsher in colour than the natural earth colours.

Van Dyke Brown is a very inferior material which has no place on the conscientious artist's palette.

Sepia is usually a simple mixture of Burnt Umber and a black.

The Palette

A summary of the paints that we have studied, together with information on mixing 'standard' colours.

Summary of the Extended Palette Mixing "Standard" Colours

Summary of the Extended Palette

All the colours we have discussed can be usefully grouped under one heading, so that their relative qualities can be considered.

Cadmium Red
Pigment Red 108

Permanence xxx. Compatible with all well produced pigments. Rather slow drying in oils. Colour varies between manufacturers. Many inferior substitutes on the market. Opaque.

Quinacridone Violet
Pigment Violet 19

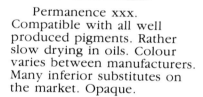

A particularly vibrant red biased toward violet.
Valued for its transparency, it gives very clear, clean washes and deep greys when combined with Phthalo Green. Syperior to Alizarin Crimson.

Rose Madder Genuine
Natural Red 9

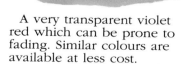

A very transparent violet red which can be prone to fading. Similar colours are available at less cost.
Very weak in mixes which limits its use. Compatible with other colours.

Quinacridone Reds

Permanence varies, up to xxxx. Wide range available. Exceptionally transparent, brilliant reds. Compatible with all other pigments. Often sold under ridiculous names such as Geranium and Rose.

Light Red Oxide
Pigment Red 101

Permanence xxxx. Compatible with other pigments. Colour varies considerably between manufacturers. Opaque with good tinting strength.

French Ultramarine
Pigment Blue 29

Permanence xxx although quickly bleached by acids such as vinegar and lemon juice. Compatible with other pigments if well made. Very transparent. High tinting strength.

Cerulean Blue
Pigment Blue 35

Permanence xxxx. Compatible with all other pigments. Student grades (and increasingly artist qualities) masquerading under this name are simple mixes of other, cheaper blues. Genuine article is excellent value. Opaque.

Cobalt Blue
Pigment Blue 28

Permanence xxxx. Compatible with all other pigments. Subject to adulteration and imitation by mixes containing cheaper blues. A unique, transparent blue.

Phthalocyanine Blue
Pigment Blue 15

Permanence xxx to xxxx. Compatible with other pigments. An extremely powerful, deep greenish blue. The various names used by manufacturers can cause unnecessary confusion. An excellent, transparent blue.

Lemon Yellow
Pigment Yellow 3
(Arylide Yellow)

Permanence xxx. A general name to describe a green yellow. Cadmium Lemon is also reliable — many others turn green. Compatible with other pigments. Transparent.

Cadmium Yellow Pale
Pigment Yellow 35

Permanence xxx to xxxx. The modern product is compatible with all pigments. Opaque but strong enough to be applied in a thin layer for a semi-transparent effect.

Aureolin (Cobalt Yellow)
Pigment Yellow 40

Permanence xxx for good makes. Compatible with all other pigments. A clear delicate colour when applied thinly. Heavy and dull laid on thickly. Particularly useful as a glaze.

Yellow Ochre
Pigment Yellow 43

Permanence xxxx. Compatible with all pigments. Quality products can be quite transparent applied thinly but the colour is usually considered to be opaque. A soft, neutral yellow.

Viridian
Pigment Green 18

Permanence xxxx. Compatible with all pigments. Use only the better grades. Highly valued as a glazing colour due to its transparency. A very bright, clear, cool green.

Phthalocyanine Green
Pigment Green 7 or
Pigment Green 36

Permanence xxx to xxxx. Compatible with other pigments. Varies from yellowish green to bluish green. A powerful colour that can dominate if not used with care. Particularly transparent.

Burnt Sienna
Pigment Brown 7

Permanence xxxx. A brilliant, rich red brown. Compatible with all other pigments. Displays its true beauty when applied thinly. An excellent glazing colour due to its transparency.

Flake White (White Lead)
Pigment White 1

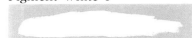

Permanence xxx. Usually only available in oils or alkyds. Compatible with all other well produced pigments. A warm, creamy white that dries to a tough flexible film. Quick drying. Opaque.

Titanium White
Pigment White 6

Permanence xxxx. Absolutely inert, unaffected by other pigments, light, heat, weak acids or alkaline. Cooler in mixes than Flake White. The whitest of the whites.

Zinc White
Pigment White 4

Permanence xxxx. A very pure, cold white. Compatible with all other pigments. In oils dries to a hard, brittle film prone to cracking. Mainly used for glazing due to its transparency.

Chinese White
Pigment White 4

Permanence xxxx. The principal white of the water colourist. Very dense, with greater covering power than the oil version. Compatible with all other pigments. Opaque.

Ivory Black
Pigment Black 9

Permanence xxxx. Colour varies from a warm brown black (applied thinly) to a dark blue black. Can be used in all techniques. Compatible with other pigments. Semi-transparent to opaque.

Mars Black
Pigment Black 11

Permanence xxxx. An excellent dense black. Varies in colour, usually a deep, warm brownish black if applied thinly. Good covering power and high in tinting strength. Fully compatible. Opaque.

Lamp Black
Pigment Black 6

Permanence xxxx. A cool bluish black. Quite high in tinting strength with excellent covering power. Compatible with other pigments. Slow drier in oils. Transparent.

Raw Umber
Pigment Brown 7

Permanence xxxx. A pleasant, cool, slightly greenish dark brown. Colour varies. Student and artist qualities equally permanent. Compatible with other pigments. Some grades fairly transparent.

Burnt Umber
Pigment Brown 7

Permanence xxxx. Compatible with all other pigments. A warm, rich, rather heavy reddish-brown. Valued for its versatility, it is considered essential by many painters. Suitable for all media.

Raw Sienna
Pigment Brown 7

Permanence xxxx. As with many other browns it is equally reliable in both student and artist qualities. Compatible with other pigments. Very transparent, it makes an excellent glazing colour.

Mixing "Standard" Colours

Many of the colours offered by paint manufacturers are simple mixes easily duplicated on the palette. Although some of them have a place as convenience colours, many are composed of materials which are unsuitable for artistic use.

If you work through the exercises as suggested, you will find that even with a limited palette you will be able to duplicate many of the colours that you might otherwise have purchased.

Some of the more common examples of pre-mixed colours are as follows:

Ultra. Blue *Cadmium Yellow*

Shown here is a typical 'Sap Green', this time mixed from reliable pigments. You will find many such greens in the colour mixing exercises.

Sap Green

A variety of Sap Greens are available, invariably made up of poor materials.

Originally made from ripened berries it is now produced from almost any concoction of blue and yellow. The materials used are invariably of poor quality, giving a very inferior paint, prone to fading or changing in some other way. It is possible, but not easy, to find a reasonably lightfast product.

The various dull greens sold under this label are easily duplicated on the palette.

Naples Yellow

Naples yellow is a convenience colour which is very easily mixed.

Genuine Naples Yellow is a lead-based pigment with some excellent properties. Drawbacks in its use (it is not suitable for water colour, pastel etc.) and difficulties in production have brought about the widespread manufacture of substitutes which are usually no more than mixes of yellows and whites.

A variety of Naples Yellows are available, all simple mixes.

In oils it is generally a mix of Cadmium Yellow and Flake White with small additions of Yellow Ochre and/or Light Red to achieve the different values that are offered.

As a water colour it is usually a mixture of Cadmium Yellow, Chinese White and Yellow Ochre. A useful convenience colour which is easily produced on the palette.

Paynes Grey

A popular, opaque blue-grey which has a soft, darkening effect on other colours. Usually produced from a combination of Ultramarine and a black. An ochre is often added to soften the colour. Another convenience paint that can easily be duplicated on the palette.

It is a colour that has to be handled carefully as it can quickly dominate and unbalance a painting.

Hookers Green

Hookers Green has become a 'dumping ground' for inferior yellows and blues.

Originally an inferior water colour paint produced from a simple mix of Prussian Blue and Gamboge. Nowadays it is still usually an inferior or at least an unnecessary pre-mixed paint available in a variety of mediums. The ingredients have changed to include almost any blue and yellow. Having checked the contributing colours used, I have come to the conclusion that the only limit is the imagination of the blender and the range of base colours available.

Hookers Green has become a dumping ground for cheap and inferior pigments. Occasionally, and almost by default, manufacturers do use better quality pigments. Any of the proprietary greens offered under this label are easily mixed.

Emerald Green

A highly poisonous substance no longer available, Genuine Emerald Green cannot be matched exactly by mixing, but a close likeness can be achieved by combining Phthalocyanine Green with Lemon Yellow. Why buy it ready mixed when you can make it yourself? The same easily prepared colour is also sold under such names as Permanent Light Green. A little white paint is sometimes added to give variation.

Sepia

Mix a little Lamp Black with Burnt Sienna and you have the same concoction as the one sold under this name.

Many other manufactured colours could be added to this list. Once you gain control over the limited palette suggested and become familiar with the other colours described, you will be able to work with far fewer colours than is the norm and be sure of their qualities. If you are ever tempted to add further colours to your range, be sure that you could not just as easily mix them.

Mixing Various Media

The laws of subtractive mixing apply to all colour blending that does not involve either coloured lights or optical mixing.

Pastels
Coloured Pencils
Silk Screen Inks
Watercolour
Gouache
Oil Paints
Acrylics
Placing Further Colours
Subtractive Mixing in Practice

Pastels

The laws of subtractive mixing apply to the use of all types of liquid paint, all inks, soft and hard pastels, oil pastels, wax crayons and coloured pencils. In fact they apply to any mixing that does not involve either coloured lights or optical blending.

Once the basic rules are understood they can be used for any suitable medium. They are not difficult guidelines to follow and their application can quickly become second nature.

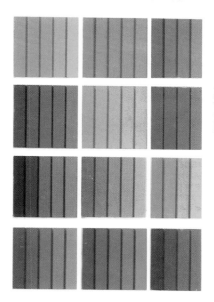

Pastel colours are not easy to combine.

Pastels are available in a very wide variety of colours, the selection of which can be extremely bewildering. The frequent use of some particularly fanciful names does not help the situation.

Neither does the fact that the ingredients and resistance to light are seldom indicated.

Hatching, or crosshatching, together with further blending by finger or torchon are the only means of mixing the colours. Such a rather awkward process makes the mixing of pastels somewhat less efficient than the mixing of liquid paints. This has led to the wide range of pre-mixed colours.

The Colour Bias Wheel can be employed as an aid in all forms of subtractive mixing.

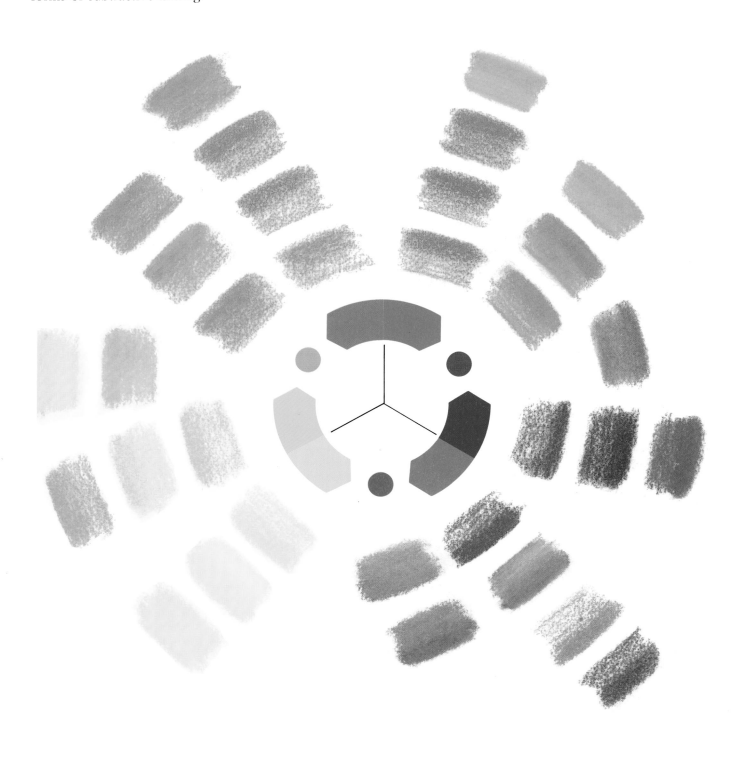

Before trying out any of the mixing exercises you should decide on the 'types' of colour that you have in your palette. Reds should be sorted out into the orange-reds and the violet-reds, blues into violet-blues and green-blues and yellows into green-yellows and orange-yellows.

Deep rose

Perm. red deep

Light yellow

Deep yellow

Many pastels have vague, meaningless names.

The bias of the red will be revealed if it is mixed with a known blue.

This test will prevent any confusion between colour 'types'.

If you are unsure of a particular colour's bias, you can soon identify it with a few sample mixes. Let's say that you have a red that is difficult to place. The name does not give a clue as to the type of red that it is and it does not appear to lean strongly in

either direction. The first thing to do is to mix it with a blue that is obviously biased towards violet. Mix the red with Ultramarine; if the result is a rather drab grey-violet you can be sure that the red is biased towards orange; if the mix is a clear violet the red

leans towards that colour and can be placed accordingly.

Other colours can be similarly arranged into 'types'.

By setting out sample colours from your palette, as shown opposite, you can always be sure of the colours to select for any given result.

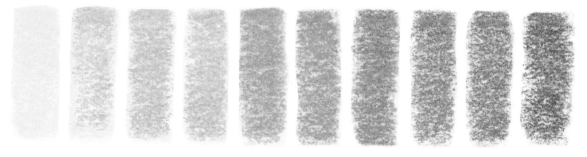

The same rules of subtractive mixing apply with pastels as they do with liquid paints.

The exercises outlined in the book should be followed, using pastels, if you are to gain total control of your palette.

Although thin applications have a certain transparency, pastels can only really be considered opaque or semi-opaque.

The usual practice is to mix pastels from dark to light.

Coloured Pencils

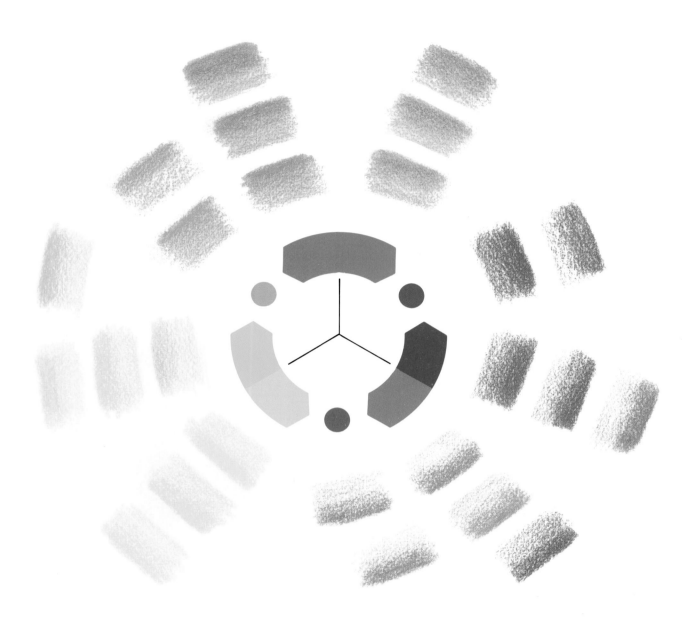

Like pastels, coloured pencils present difficulties when it comes to combining colours. Hatching, or crosshatching must be employed. Nevertheless, a good range of delicate, subtle results can be obtained from just a few colours.

Coloured pencils are even more vaguely labelled than pastels — if they are given a colour name at all.

Once again, it would be of great benefit to arrange your selection according to each colour's bias. As with the pastels, a few trial mixes will enable you to classify colours according to 'type'.

When you have decided on each colour's bias, you will learn a great deal by working through the exercises in the book.

Regardless of the medium, complementaries can be relied on to neutralise each other, thanks to the laws of subtractive mixing.

Silk Screen Inks

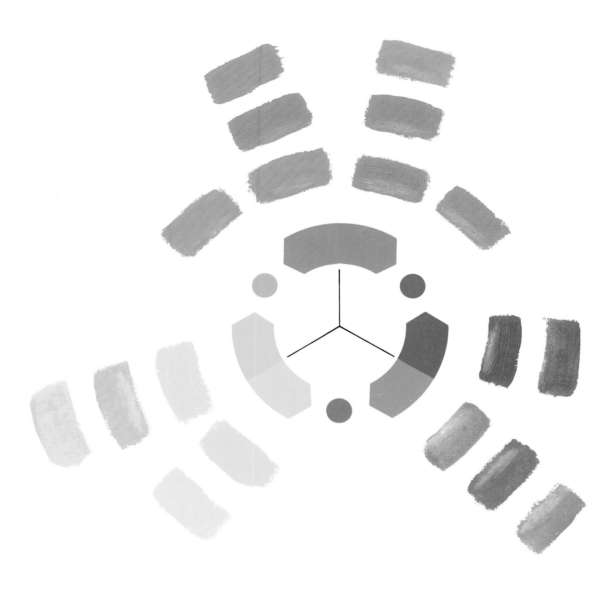

Nomenclature of silk screen inks varies considerably between manufacturers. Some name their colours to correspond with the more familiar titles of the painter's materials, others use exotic, meaningless names.

Rather than try to make sense of the labels, spend your time arranging the colours according to their biases. The yellows and blues are usually quite easy to place by sight alone. If in doubt, try a little experimenting.

1

The yellow that combines with a greenish blue to give a dull green obviously leans towards orange and should be placed accordingly.

2

If a bright green results, place the yellow in the 'Lemon Yellow' position on the wheel.

Reds are often the most difficult to judge by sight. If the container is labelled say, Magic Red Number 3 and you cannot confidently decide on its leaning, mix a little with a known violet-blue. If a greyed violet results then you know that Magic Red Number 3 is similar in character to a Cadmium Red. It is biased towards orange. If a bright violet results then you have a red leaning towards that hue on your hands.

3

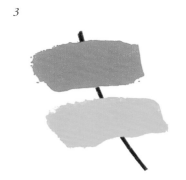

Whether oil or water-based, most screen inks are opaque when they are applied heavily.

4

Either by thinning or through adding a special base, the inks can be made transparent.

5

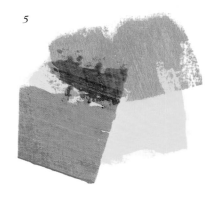

Overprinting with transparent inks produces further colours.

6

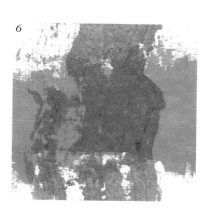

The rules of subtractive mixing are applicable whether the colours are physically mixed or applied as glazes.

7

Complementaries will still darken each other and produce greys when they are evenly combined.

8

A knowledge of the six colour 'types' is essential. An orange yellow and a violet blue make a dull green in screen inks no matter how they are combined.

Watercolour

Fortunately, the nomenclature of watercolours is uniform between manufacturers. Although some rather meaningless names are still widely used, they are reserved for the less important colours.

If you have colours other than those so far examined, their bias should be ascertained first before they are used.

One of the great beauties of watercolour painting is the ease with which different techniques can be combined.

Wet into wet, wet on dry, glazing etc. In order to take advantage of this flexibility the painter must have full control over colour mixing and a clear understanding of the characteristics of each colour. The differences in transparency in particular should be noted.

Note:
As all of the exercises in the book were carried out using watercolours, the bias of the major colours should be well established.

Staining Colours

Certain pigments possess phenomenal strength and must be used with caution. These are the staining colours, they will stain both the paper and other pigments.

Once applied they are impossible to remove and difficult to alter. Although they can be used to provide deep but thin darks, their ability to stain other colours can be a distinct disadvantage.

Colours such as Phthalocyanine Blue and Green fall into this category.

Staining Test

Apply a small patch of each colour to be tested onto the same type of paper as you normally use.

After the paint has dried, soften it with a clean wet brush.

Remove the paint by either running the paper under a tap or by washing it with a very wet sponge.

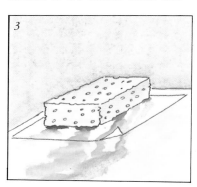

Once the paper has dried it is easy to identify the staining colours.

Gouache

Gouache, also known as 'Designers Colour', is simply opaque watercolour. Standard watercolours are made opaque by the addition of either white paint or an inert pigment such as precipitated chalk.

Available in tubes, jars, pans and cakes, gouache is used extensively by commercial artists since its opacity makes it very suitable for reproduction.

The smooth texture and opacity of gouache is attracting an increasing number of painters working in the field of fine art, painters who all too often do not realise the limitations of this medium.

Manufactured primarily for the graphic artist, the gouache range includes many bright but fugitive colours. The work of the commercial artist is, for the most part, kept away from light in a folder and is not usually intended for an especially long life.

If you choose to work in gouache, pay attention to the manufacturer's literature and select only the lightfast colours.

Although many are lightfast, some gouache paints can fade so much that only a trace of colour remains, even after a short exposure.

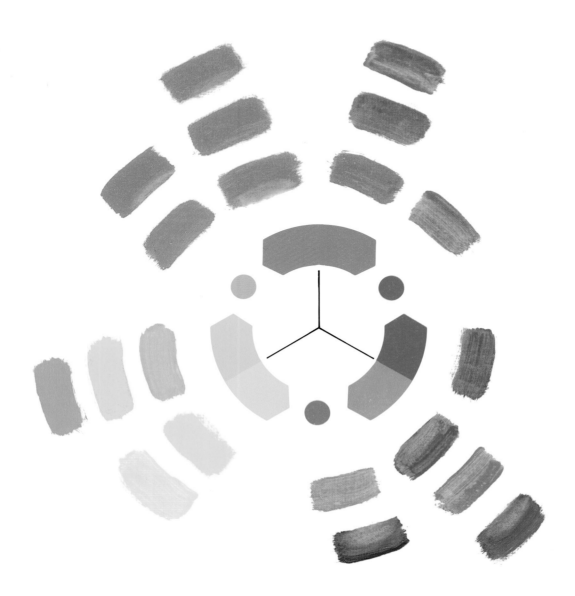

Once the bias of a colour has been established, whether by sight or by experimenting, position it around the bias wheel.

1

As with any medium, the bias of an oil colour can be confirmed quickly by a simple test. If you are unsure of a yellow, for example, mix it with a known orange red such as Cadmium Red.

2

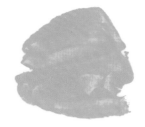

If the result is a bright orange then the yellow is biased towards orange. If the mix is a rather drab colour then the yellow is obviously biased towards green and should be used as such.

3

Some yellows however are rather weak and easily swamped by the red. Should this be the case, the bias may be more difficult to establish.

4

As a further test mix the yellow with a green blue such as Cerulean Blue.

5

If the resulting green is dull it follows that the yellow is biased towards orange.

6

If it is bright then the yellow must lean towards green.

Slow drying oil paints lend themselves to the technique of painting wet into wet, the colours being mixed on the painting surface rather than on the palette.

This method of mixing can produce very fresh, sparkling results due to the partial blending of the paints.

Without a clear understanding of colour mixing this approach is invariably disastrous. Instead of fresh, spontaneous results, the work looks very muddy. An intended bright violet, for example, is destroyed by the use of an orange red, or through the inclusion of a little yellow paint. Likewise a fresh green can turn dark should Ultramarine or a tiny amount of red be added.

When you understand colour mixing, the technique of mixing directly on the canvas will be at your disposal.

Acrylics

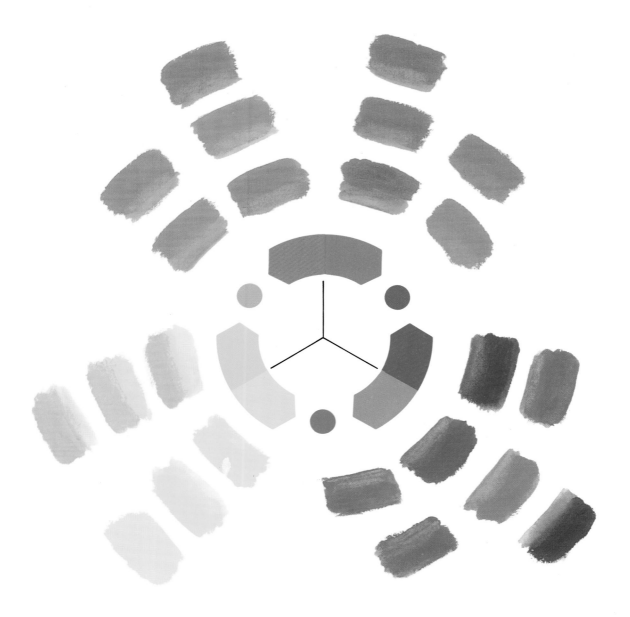

Many of the traditional pigments used in oil and watercolour paints are also available in acrylics, a medium recently introduced. To these have been added an extensive range of modern synthetic colours of great strength and brilliance. Many of these relatively new colours are particularly transparent, making them ideal glazing colours. Shown here is a typical range of acrylic colours.

The speed with which acrylic paints dry can be an advantage in some respects though it makes colour blending very difficult and virtually rules out the technique of mixing directly on the painting surface.

In order to slow the drying rate, a retarding medium can be added to the paint. Colour blending becomes possible but

overuse of the retarder makes the paint more transparent, a quality not always wanted.

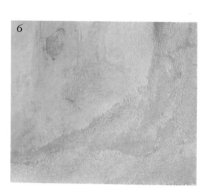

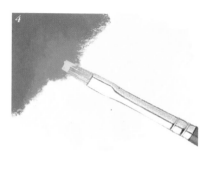

To reduce this tendency towards transparency and to make colour mixing on the surface possible, the retarder medium can be applied directly to the area to be painted and the colours worked into it.

Where transparency is required, a gel medium can be added to the paint. The drawback, however, is some loss of intensity (red moves towards pink for example).

Acrylics darken slightly as they dry but with experience you can allow for this.

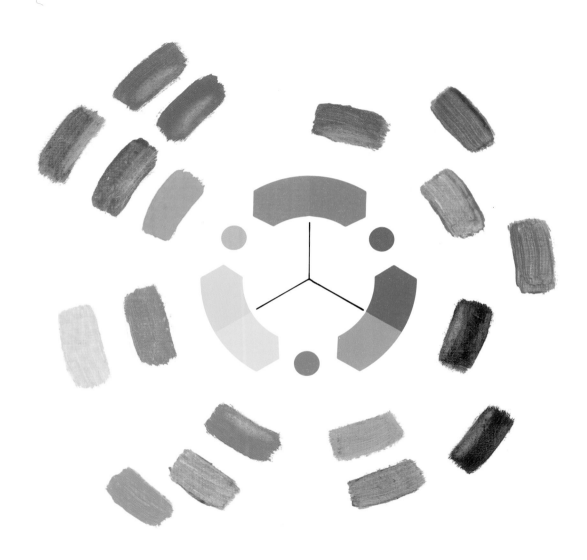

The bias wheel accommodates any colour except black and white and once you are familiar with its use and can place any red, yellow or blue according to its bias, any additional colours you may wish to use can also be positioned.

Manufactured greens, oranges and violets can be categorised quite easily by eye.

The differences between blue violets and red violets, for example, are usually obvious. If in doubt the colour can be placed in the centre, halfway between the red and blue positions.

The duller hues such as Naples Yellow and Light Red are a little more difficult to decide upon. An exact positioning is less important in

their case as such colours have a relatively minor role to play.

Shown here are just some of the colours that can usually be found in an oil painter's box. This is not to suggest they are necessarily useful, suitable or could not easily be mixed. Such decisions will be yours to make.

Once you have categorised the colours you intend to use, the decisions about how to use them follow easily.

For example, Yellow Ochre can now be considered a neutralized orange yellow rather than as a nondescript yellowish brown.

Mixed with Cadmium Red it produces a soft, neutral, opaque orange.

With Cerulean Blue a gentle, dull, opaque green emerges.

Moving across the wheel, Yellow Ochre can be used to neutralize (and make less transparent), a violet mixed from Quinacridone Violet and Ultramarine Blue.

If Burnt Sienna is treated as a neutralized transparent orange rather than a type of brown, it will become a much more versatile colour.

If can be used to darken a transparent blue such as Ultramarine.

Or glazed over Lemon Yellow to provide a slightly neutral transparent orange.

An opaque mid-green such as Oxide of Chromium can be moved towards blue with Cerulean Blue or moved

towards blue and dulled at the same time with Ultramarine Blue.

Subtractive Mixing in Practice

The aim of this book has been to provide information which will enable the reader to turn colour mixing from a haphazard affair, shrouded in myth, into a thinking process.

Once the basic rules of subtractive mixing are fully understood, their application, after a little practice, will quickly become second nature. We can reduce these rules to the following:

1. In mixing bright, clear violets, oranges or greens, select contributing colours that both carry the same bias as the one you require. For example, if both the yellow and the blue are biased towards green, they will mix into a pure green.

2. In order to produce a dull or neutralized violet, orange or green, select contributing colours that are inefficient 'carriers' of that colour. For instance, using a blue that leans towards violet dulls an otherwise bright green. The colour can be further dulled by introducing a yellow biased towards orange.

3. To neutralize any colour, add its complementary (red to green for example).

4. Greys can be produced by evenly mixing a complementary pair, such as red and green.

Colour mixing should be a thinking process based on knowledge.

By understanding the processes that take place within the paint film, a colour can quickly be taken in any direction you choose.

As an example, let's take a red with a bias towards orange, such as the painter's Cadmium Red.

It can be moved towards bright orange by adding an 'orange'-yellow.

Made into a dull orange with a 'greenish'-yellow.

Slightly darkened and softened with a red biased towards violet.

Moved towards a dull violet with a 'violet'-blue.

Towards an even duller violet with a blue biased towards green.

Neutralised with a green.

With a little thought and practice, any colour can be manipulated in this fashion.

Let others buy, use and waste needless colours. Spend more time mixing than applying colours and then be obliged to work with a very restricted range.

You now have the information to gain total control over your palette. Your work can only improve.

Taken towards grey with green.

Turned into a 'dusky' pink by adding white to create a tint and green to dull that colour. And on it goes.

Other Titles

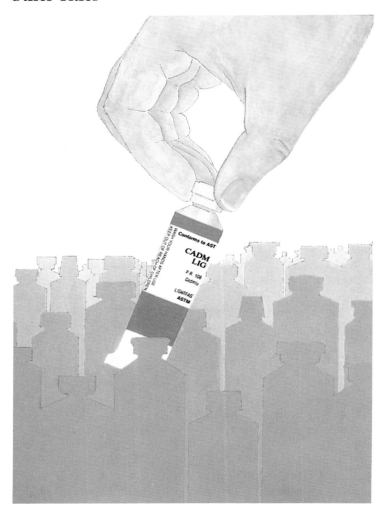

The Wilcox Guide to the Best Watercolor Paints

This is a landmark book for artists. It contains a surprising amount of information that is not available elsewhere.

Equally important, the information is presented in a handsome, easily referenced format. No matter how knowledgeable you are as an artist, you are going to be surprised by some of the facts in this book. It is the first publication to cover the wide range of pigments currently used in artists' watercolours, many of them almost unknown in the art community. In fact, it is the first to completely document the pigments used in any artists' medium.

This book summarizes what is known about these pigments and gives the watercolours that contain each pigment. The major watercolour manufacturers around the world are covered, along with a thumbnail sketch of the individual companies. No matter where you live some of the brands described in the book will be available. Colour reproductions of each watercolour coupled with a description of its handling qualities, add another essential piece of information. The guidance on colour mixing is a bonus.

It was a herculean task to gather, evaluate and compile this information, and even more difficult to present it in a practical form, as Michael Wilcox has done. When I heard his plan for this book I realized how valuable it would be, but wondered if it would be possible to acquire the necessary information and put it together in one manageable book. It is a great pleasure to see what can be accomplished through courage, determination and skill.

The pigment used in a paint determines how long the colour will last. It is also the most expensive ingredient in a paint, so there is a strong economic incentive for companies to use the less expensive pigments. Sometimes this works to the artist's advantage since the best pigments are not always the most expensive ones, but it can also lead to use of inferior pigments.

Knowledge on the part of artists counter balances this pressure. The more knowledgeable you are, the better supplies you will have.

The art teacher and the artist buying paints, have been looking at a giant jigsaw puzzle with most of its pieces missing.

Michael Wilcox has supplied those pieces. This book provides the tools to safeguard your work and to reform the industry. Companies will supply what artists will buy.

Joy Turner Luke

Chairwoman, Artist Equity Association Materials Research Committee. Former Chairwoman, American Society for Testing & Materials Subcommittee on Artists' Paints. Former member of U.S. Bureau of Standards Committee on Artists' Paints. Past President Inter-Society Colour Council

(Extract from the foreword)

Available at all good bookstores or from the 'School of Colour'.

ISBN 0 89134 409 8

U.K. Title. 'The Wilcox Guide to the Finest Watercolour Paints'.

The Michael Wilcox Palette

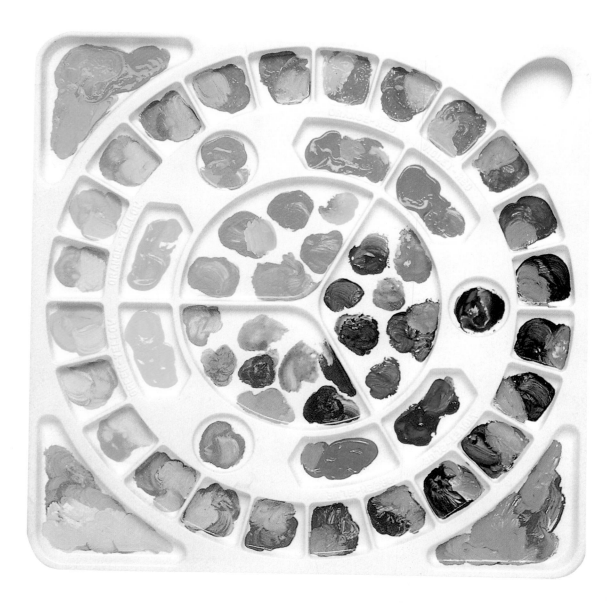

A Colour Mixing Palette, based on the Colour Bias Wheel, has been designed to give constant guidance on the colours to select for accurate mixing.

The palette is the practical extension to the methods outlined in this book and quickly gives total control,

regardless of the type of paint or ink used.

There are two types of palette, one for water soluble colours, the other for oil based.

Available only through the School of Colour. Please see next page.

Paints

If you should experience difficulty in obtaining any of the colours used throughout this book, we can now help.

A range of twelve colours has been designed with mixing and reliability in mind. All are lightfast and fully compatible.

Available in Watercolours - Oils - Acrylics - Artists Gouache and Designers Gouache.

For further information contact the School of Colour.

The School of Colour

Following the initial release of this book, it soon became apparent that there was a demand for further information on colour use and understanding.

We have found that Colour Theory, Harmony and Contrast have often been poorly explained. To the extent that most people who work with colour do so in confusion.

To help overcome this situation we have produced a series of practical courses which provide thorough training in each area.

If you would like further information on our courses, palettes or paints please contact:

The Michael Wilcox School of Colour USA.
P.O.Box 1399
Tellevast. FL 34270
Fax: 813 351 7406
Tel: 813 355 7150

The Michael Wilcox School of Colour U.K.
P.O. Box 3518
London SE24 9LW
Fax: 071 274 9160
Tel: 071 738 7751

The Michael Wilcox School of Colour Australia.
P.O. Box 358 Kelmscott
Western Australia 6111
Fax: (09) 390 5936
Tel: (09) 466 1053